NO-SEW COSPLAY MADE EASY

NO-SEW COSPLAY MADE EASY

EVERYTHING YOU NEED TO DRESS AS YOUR FAVORITE CHARACTERS

KEN AND KADE
DinoBunny Cosplay

Copyright © 2025 Kennedy and Kaden Witten

First published in 2025 by
Page Street Publishing Co.
27 Congress Street, Suite 1511
Salem, MA 01970
www.pagestreetpublishing.com

All rights reserved. No part of this book may be reproduced or used, in any form or by any means, electronic or mechanical, without prior permission in writing from the publisher.

Distributed by Macmillan, sales in Canada by The Canadian Manda Group.

29 28 27 26 25   1 2 3 4 5

ISBN-13: 979-8-89003-208-9

Library of Congress Control Number: 2024933715

Edited by Elliot Wren Phillips
Cover and book design by Laura Benton for Page Street Publishing Co.
Photography by Kennedy and Kaden Witten

Printed and bound in the United States of America

Page Street Publishing protects our planet by donating to nonprofits like The Trustees, which focuses on local land conservation.

DEDICATION

To those who have been taught to be ashamed of who they are. Who have to fight to be seen, heard, or simply allowed to exist: This book is for you.

May your light continue to shine in the darkness of a world still learning to see.

CONTENTS

Introduction 9

COSPLAYING A CHARACTER 11

Choosing Your Character 12
Breaking Down a Character's Design for Cosplay 13
Creating Your Own Original Design for a Character 14

WIG? SNATCHED 17

What Kind of Wig Should I Buy? 18
Types of Wigs 19
Wig Quality Red Flags 20
How to Wear a Wig 21
   Tutorial: How to Put on a Wig 23
Wig Styling Basics 25
   Tutorial: Trimming Bangs to Suit Your Face 26
   Tutorial: Adding Volume 29
   Tutorial: Curling Wigs 30
   Tutorial: Creating a Formed Spike on a Wig 33
   Tutorial: Dyeing a Wig 37
Wig Maintenance and Storage 38

PAINTING YOUR FACE! 41

Study Your Features 42
Getting Your Face Ready for Makeup 45
Basic Makeup Techniques 46
   Tutorial: Changing the Color of a Long Beard 54
   Tutorial: Changing the Color of a Short or Sparse Beard 57
   Tutorial: Covering a Beard 58
Drag Makeup 61
SFX Looks 80
   Tutorial: Applying a Water-Activated Body Paint 83
   Tutorial: Aging Yourself with Makeup 84
   Tutorial: Scar Makeup 88
   Tutorial: Ghost Makeup 91

FABRIC AND FRILLS — 97

Buying Costumes — 98
Customizing Fabric Color — 99
- Tutorial: Stovetop Dyeing — 101
- Tutorial: Ombré Dyeing — 102
- Tutorial: Dyeing a Full Garment in the Washing Machine — 104
- Tutorial: Dyeing Real Leather — 106
- Tutorial: Creating Small Symbols with Fabric Paint — 109
- Tutorial: Adding Ombré Details with Fabric Paint — 110

Iron-Ons — 112
- Tutorial: Fabric Transfers — 113
- Tutorial: Patches — 115
- Tutorial: Iron-On Vinyl — 116

Weathering — 119
- Tutorial: Weathering Fake Leather — 120

Adding Spikes — 123
- Tutorial: Customizing Leather with Spikes — 124

Customizing Footwear — 126
- Tutorial: Gems, Bows, and More — 127
- Tutorial: Glitter — 129
- Tutorial: Adding Ribbon — 130
- Tutorial: Painting Footwear — 133

THE KITCHEN SINK! (EVERYTHING ELSE) — 135

Basic Foam Work — 136
Patterning Foam Props — 137
- Tutorial: Making a Crown — 139
- Tutorial: Making Your Own Spike Template — 143
- Tutorial: How to Make a Foam Spike — 146
- Tutorial: Customizing Premade Horns — 149
- Tutorial: Customizing a Prop Sword — 153
- Tutorial: Animal Ears — 158

A Final Word — 163
Acknowledgments — 164
About the Authors — 165
Index — 166

INTRODUCTION

If you're picking up this book, you might be familiar with the word "cosplay." But what does it really mean? Is it just dressing up? Acting? Crafting? Role-playing?

The short answer is that it's all of the above! Cosplay is short for costume play, the hobby of dressing up as characters from pop culture such as games, movies, or TV shows! There are no rules or boundaries, so there are truly endless possibilities for what you do as a cosplayer. Cosplayers often showcase their creations at conventions, meetups, photo shoots, or in their own online communities. A lot of cosplayers either make or alter their own costumes from scratch. Some of these cosplays are simple and fun, while others are intricate pieces for competing in contests!

People ask us every day, "Do you have tips for new cosplayers?" This book is intended to give people the basics of cosplay without having to use a sewing machine. Whether you are new to cosplay or are an experienced cosplayer searching for new techniques, we hope we can spark your creativity and inspire you to make amazing things.

With so many different ways to cosplay, starting out is extremely overwhelming! This book breaks cosplay down into different aspects for you to choose from on your own cosplay journey.

OUR COSPLAY JOURNEY

We're DinoBunny Cosplay, short-form video creators and professional cosplayers. As a married couple, we're incredibly lucky to have a strong mixed skill set to help us with our creative passions.

I'm Ken! I've been cosplaying on and off since 2010. I grew up in a small town in California. My family didn't have a lot of money growing up, so learning to craft and create cosplays using unconventional materials was a huge part of my creative process! In 2021, I really started homing in on a signature cosplay style, taking huge inspiration from iconic drag artists. As an adult, I started focusing on wig styling and makeup.

I'm Kade. I cosplayed for the first time in 2003, but I really started taking an interest in 2019 with the rise of short-form videos. I have a Bachelor of Fine Arts degree in visual effects and animation. Cosplaying quickly became a creative outlet for me to learn new skills and to exercise my video background. I especially am confident with sculpting, wig styling, painting and SFX makeup.

COSPLAYING A CHARACTER

It's an incredible feeling looking into the mirror and realizing you have brought one of your favorite characters to life. Choosing a character and breaking down their design to make this possible is an important first step of any cosplay project.

CHOOSING YOUR CHARACTER

While many cosplayers already have a laundry list of "cosplans," new cosplayers might feel overwhelmed and stuck. Everyone has limited time and limited resources, which is why you should choose a character you're truly excited about! When you think about cosplay, which part excites you the most? Is it wigs, makeup, or armor? Be sure to choose a character you will enjoy creating and wearing!

You might feel pressure to choose a character you look like. While this is a valid option, I strongly recommend choosing a character you love! It can be incredibly rewarding to see yourself transform into a character you're passionate about. Cosplay is supposed to be fun! Never feel pressured into thinking it should be a look-alike contest.

When I choose new cosplays, I often base it on convenience. A red wig is on sale? I'll cosplay Jessica Rabbit *(Who Framed Roger Rabbit)*! I happen to have a red blazer in my closet? I'll cosplay Charlie Morningstar *(Hazbin Hotel)*!

BREAKING DOWN A CHARACTER'S DESIGN FOR COSPLAY

What makes a character recognizable? Is it their hair? Their makeup? Their costume? Their prop? When you are cosplaying a character, be sure to identify the most identifiable feature of their design. This characteristic should be the focus of the costume.

Let's use Princess Peach as an example. Regardless of what costume she is wearing, she is always identifiable by her eye-catching bangs, her golden crown, and her iconic pink lips. By focusing on her most identifiable design traits, you can be flexible and creative for the rest of the cosplay. The first time I cosplayed Princess Peach, I focused on these three design features and wore a pink Lolita dress I happened to have in my closet.

This strategy can be transferred to almost any cosplay. Look at your favorite character and pick out their most iconic design features. For Link (*Legend of Zelda*) this could be the Hylian crest and his famous green hat. For Kagamine Rin (*Vocaloid*) this could be her white bow and unique hair. Try it for yourself. Which features of your favorite character stand out to you the most?

CREATING YOUR OWN ORIGINAL DESIGN FOR A CHARACTER

Some characters, such as nonhuman characters, objects, or even concepts, are so abstract they might be more difficult to turn into a wearable costume. However, these monsters and animals leave a lot of room for creative freedom. With these blank-slate characters it's important to focus on both their physical traits as well as their personalities.

King Boo (*Super Mario Bros.*) is a fairly easy original design to conceptualize. He has a crown. He is a ghost. He is a king. For our human design for King Boo, we created the crown ourselves (page 139) and gave him white hair. His attire is regal and formal, emphasizing his title, "King Boo."

There are some instances where fashion and cosplay can overlap. For Kade's Monokuma cosplay (page 10), he was challenged to transform a bear whose body is split down the center into two different colored parts: Its right side is white, while its left side is black. The only other defining physical characteristic of this character is the unique shape of his red right eye. Kade took the antagonistic concept of this character and translated the design into a punk-inspired fashion look.

Even though these costumes look quite different from the original character, they are still recognizable and translate well as original designs. Costumes like this can often be more budget friendly than trying to create a one-to-one recreation of a character with a very specific design.

COSPLAY AND GENDER

Cosplay is a powerful tool for gender expression. It doesn't matter who the character is, what gender they are, or what gender *you* are. Dressing up is something anyone can do in any way they please. Using costumes and makeup creatively can be incredibly euphoric, and making creative design choices for your cosplay can be empowering.

When I (Ken) first started cosplaying, I did not feel comfortable in cosplays of feminine characters. I solely cosplayed male characters, and I would do something called "gender-bending" female characters when I cosplayed them for my own comfortability. When I started cosplaying female characters again, I started approaching makeup similarly to how drag queens approach their own makeup. This inspired me to experiment and feel comfortable enough to branch out as a cosplayer, creating the unique style we've developed today.

While the term "gender-bend" might not be as popular anymore, there is nothing stopping anyone from cosplaying their favorite character with a different gender design than the source material. Cosplay is art, and as an artist you have all the freedom in the world to express yourself how you see fit.

WIG? SNATCHED

Wig styling isn't black and white. There are many ways to go about it. The majority of styling is about working with what you have. Understanding the basics of wig styling can completely alter your results! There will always be something new to learn, and that is part of the magic! These basic skills can help you level up your wig styling game.

WHAT KIND OF WIG SHOULD I BUY?

It truly depends on the character! Imagine the design of the character in your head. Are you cosplaying a character with long hair or short hair? Is the character's hair slicked back or are their bangs covering their forehead? Do they have a ponytail? Do they have pigtails? Does their hair consist of unconventional materials? These are all factors to keep in mind while shopping for wigs. Think of how the character's hair looks and pick wigs based on that. Don't feel limited to wigs that are specifically marketed for the character you're cosplaying.

One of the most popular and reputable sites for cosplay wigs is Arda Wigs. Arda's wigs are high-heat resistant and high density and are perfect for dramatic styling. We've found the texture of the wigs to be softer and less irritating on the skin than some other brands. Their shorter wigs are around $30, but their longer and lace front wigs can get very expensive. They have a ton of options for colors and styles, but unfortunately can often be out of stock.

Other cosplay wigs sites we've been happy with have been Epic Cosplay, The Five Wits Wigs, and Kasou Wig. We will often check these sites to see if they have more affordable options than Arda or if Arda is out of stock. Sites that are more oriented toward fashion wigs can also have great options for cosplay. For lace front wigs, we like the fashion wig brands Wig Is Fashion and Weekendwigs. I've also bought wigs on Amazon, but the quality can be very hit or miss. We tend to only buy off Amazon for time-sensitive projects that require fast shipping. The pictures on Amazon can be misleading, so make sure to check buyer reviews to see what they say.

Balancing "What can I afford?" with "Will this wig suit my needs?" will lead you to more success. Sometimes it can be worth paying a few extra dollars for a wig that will be easier to work with. Wig prices can vary from around $10 to over $100. Most of our quality wigs are between $30 and $80. While a cheaper wig may be tempting, you may end up regretting it if it's not the proper quality. I've rolled the dice on low-price-tag wigs and was extremely disappointed. Occasionally, I'll strike gold and find a wig that's both very affordable and high quality. What's more common is that the low price will reflect a wig that is low quality. I'll try to make the cheap wig work, but will need to inevitably replace it due to quality issues. I end up spending more money than I would've if I just bought the nicer wig from the get-go.

TYPES OF WIGS

There are a few types of wigs you will encounter often on your cosplay journey. The most common type is wigs with bangs. These are very simple to style and dye, and they're the most affordable!

If you need a character's hair to be slicked back or you want their hairline to look incredibly natural, you might want a lace front wig. Lace front wigs are much more expensive, but if worn correctly, they can drastically improve the quality of a cosplay.

Some characters might have a ponytail or even pigtails! There are a few different ways to achieve this style. We highly recommend that beginners start out by using clip-on ponytails for these characters. Keep in mind that if you choose to wear a wig with a long ponytail in the back, the wig will be weighed down and may start to slip and fall. It's important to use bobby pins, glue, and even elastic headbands underneath the wig to keep it in place throughout the day!

Wig with regular bangs

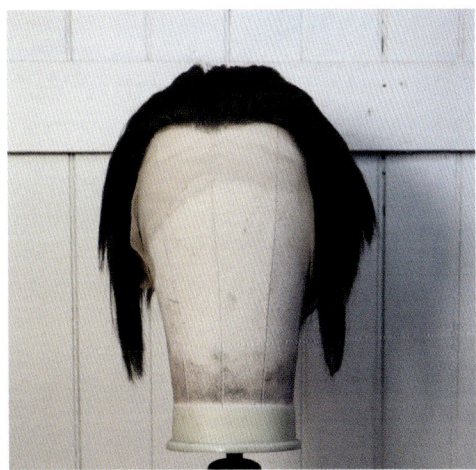
Lace front wig

Clip-on ponytails

WIG QUALITY RED FLAGS

One of the biggest giveaways of a low-quality wig is an extremely shiny texture. The extreme shine on the wig will make it look more synthetic and unrealistic. There are tricks to reduce the shine, such as a sprinkling the wig with baby powder. However, that's just putting a Band-Aid on a bigger problem. Shiny wigs are typically made with low-quality fibers that aren't heat resistant. This will severely limit your options for styling. If a wig isn't heat resistant, it might melt when using essential heat tools. Low-quality fibers will also tangle easily, suffer from breakage, and won't last as long. Typically, it's best to avoid buying a shiny wig.

Another issue to watch out for is wig density. Wigs that are too thick can be trimmed with thinning scissors. However, wigs that are too thin are often unsalvageable. Wigs are made using something called wefts. These are lines of woven hair fibers sewn into the base of the wig to form what looks like a head of hair. If these wefts are too spaced out or thin, you can see the seams of the wefts through the hair. The back of the wig is often where the density will be the worst.

I once had a wig like this. I could make it look good from the front, but if I turned around, the wig was so thin the wefts were showing. You know there is a problem when you look like you're balding *after* putting on a wig. I wasn't able to create my usual gravity-defying style to the back of the head at all, because parting the hair highlighted the big gaps in the wefts. The wig was only useful for filming front-view videos, and I wouldn't be caught dead wearing it to a convention. When I finally replaced it with a higher density wig, I could feel my confidence in my cosplay skyrocket.

HOW TO WEAR A WIG

It might seem obvious, but wearing a wig properly is step one of elevating the quality of your cosplay when you are first starting out. You want to make sure your wig is fully covering your real hair and in a position that looks natural. You don't want the wig to be sitting on your head like a hat.

A wig cap is beneficial for holding your hair in place when wearing a wig. Wig caps help smooth out unwanted bumps caused by your natural hair. You might think that a wig cap is unnecessary if you have short hair, but we recommend still wearing one. Once I didn't wear a wig cap after getting a buzz cut. I quickly realized how unpleasant the wig felt against my bare scalp. The wig cap also provides a layer of friction against the wig that helps with grip. Wig caps also help keep your wigs clean so you don't have to wash them as often. The most common types of wig caps are nylon and mesh caps; which one you use is mainly a matter of personal preference.

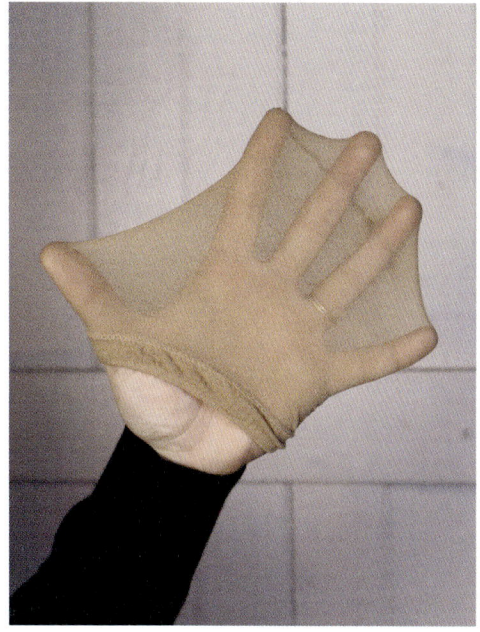

Nylon wig cap

Nylon caps are made of stocking or pantyhose-like material. This type of wig cap provides a snug fit to help keep natural hair in place. The nylon cap also prevents hair from touching the wig netting itself, which helps to keep the wigs clean. These caps can be somewhat looser, which can be better for those who are sensitive to tension around the head. Some people like to use bobby pins on the edges to help keep the cap extra secure.

Mesh caps are made of fishnet material. They have the benefit of allowing more air to pass through the cap to the scalp, which is great for those who get hot easily. They also tend to have a thicker band, which can add more security.

For lace front wigs, there are extreme-hold wig glues and more extensive methods for adhering wigs. These methods are meant for long-term wear. If you're new to wigs, use these methods with caution. Long-term wig glues require specific products to remove. Trying to remove them with just water and brute force is a bad idea. You can damage your skin, natural hair, and the wig itself.

Fortunately to those new to lace fronts, these long-term-hold wig glues are unnecessary for most cosplay. The majority of cosplayers wear their wigs for less than eight hours, so long-term wear adhesives aren't needed. A better option for beginners is a glueless lace gel such as Bold Hold Liquid Gold.

Mesh wig cap

TUTORIAL

HOW TO PUT ON A WIG

Make sure that when you first put on your wig, it is properly attached to your head for the best results. Wearing your wig well will make all the difference.

WHAT YOU WILL NEED

Wig cap

Wig

Wig glue (optional)

1. To properly put on a wig cap, first choose a nylon or mesh wig cap. As someone with short hair, I prefer using nylon bald caps because they're more comfortable for me. If you have long or thick hair, you might need to use a mesh wig cap underneath as well. Make sure to pre-stretch your wig caps to avoid getting a headache. We do this by gripping the wig cap with both hands and slowly stretching it for a few minutes. Put on your wig cap.

2. Next, adjust the size of the wig using the hooks in the back of the wig. Most wigs come with size adjusters. Always use these to make a wig fit comfortably. If you have a larger head, make sure to clip these onto the loosest setting to avoid them popping undone.

3. Put the wig on by holding it to the forehead first. Then pull the back over the wig cap, carefully avoiding your natural hair.

4. You can also glue the wig down for extra security. This is an optional step, but we find it can really help keep the sideburn sections of wigs in place throughout the day and really makes a difference in photos.

(continued)

HOW TO PUT ON A WIG (CONTINUED)

5. For wig sideburns, we prefer to use Bold Hold Liquid Gold, a glueless adhesion product that is specifically made for short-term wear. This product has strong adhesion, won't damage your wig, and can be removed without any special products. Eyelash glue can also work, but keep in mind eyelash glue can be very difficult to get out of wigs. To apply any kind of wig adhesion, use the following steps:

- Remove makeup from the part of the face the wig will be glued to. If you glue the wig on top of your makeup, the glue won't actually be touching your skin and will come off easily. The makeup might also alter the color of your wig.

- Apply a thin layer of glue to the skin and spread evenly.

- Dry until tacky. Do not apply the wig to wet glue or it won't stick.

- Press the sideburn/wig fiber onto the glue and hold until dry.

WIG STYLING BASICS

Every cosplayer should have some understanding of basic wig styling, even if it is just trimming the bangs of a wig. We highly recommend buying wigs that are as close to the haircut of the character as possible. Cutting a very long wig to be very short in the back is extremely difficult, and in some cases impossible due to the spacing of the wefts. Here is a breakdown of some of the supplies you might use for basic wig styling.

Wig heads: Styrofoam wig heads are much smaller than human heads. If you are performing any wig styling on a Styrofoam wig head, keep in mind the wig will look *much* shorter on most human heads. For this reason, we prefer to use canvas wig heads for all wig styling. You can find these for under $25.

Hairspray: Regular hairspray is not intended to be used on synthetic wig fibers. Most cosplayers use göt2b® glued® for styling wigs due to its strong hold and long-lasting effect. We recommend getting this hairspray.

Scissors: Getting proper hair-cutting scissors is strongly recommended. They are sharper, and can cut with more precise detail. That being said, we have used crafting scissors and kitchen shears in a pinch. No judgment here.

Steamer: The steamer we use is meant for fabric and was $20 on Amazon. Getting a fancy steamer is unnecessary. **Never use a steamer while someone is wearing the wig, as it can cause severe burns.**

Hair crimper: Any hair crimper with custom heat settings will work. A lot of cheaper wigs will melt under extreme heat. Even heat-resistant wigs should not be heated more than 350°F (175°C). In a pinch, you can use a flat iron for any steps in which we recommend using a hair crimper. A hair crimper will result in more volume.

Silicone-based detangling spray: Most detanglers meant for human hair use conditioner to detangle, which won't be as effective on synthetic fibers. Get a silicone-based detangler. Check the ingredients on any detangler before buying. We recommend Mane 'n Tail® detangler since it's easy to find at most stores.

Comb: Having a pick at the end of the comb makes it much easier to separate sections of the wig to work with. If there isn't a comb with a pick available, chopsticks will also work!

Synthetic fabric dye: Never use hair dye on a synthetic wig. The most popular brand of synthetic fabric dye is Rit® fabric dye. Always use synthetic fabric dye rather than all-purpose.

In the next few pages, we'll go over some essential wig-styling tips that can really elevate your look and streamline the process!

TUTORIAL

TRIMMING BANGS TO SUIT YOUR FACE

Wigs with bangs are commonly used in anime cosplay. Even if a wig *looks* pre-styled, we can almost always guarantee some trimming will be necessary to achieve the desired result. It's important to know basic cutting techniques even if you don't plan on doing heavy styling! Having a wig trimmed to fit your face is a simple way to elevate your cosplay.

Cutting wigs is *not* like cutting human hair. You shouldn't cut straight across. Instead, you need to hold your scissors at a 90-degree angle to the hair. Remember, you can always cut more, but you cannot add hair back on. When cutting the wig, proceed slowly. If you are trimming a wig to fit your face, it's far more effective to wear the wig or have someone else help you.
Note: Trimming bangs when the wig is on a wig head might result in the bangs being far too short.

WHAT YOU WILL NEED

Comb with a pick

Scissors

Hairspray (optional)

1. Using your comb, brush through the wig thoroughly, removing any tangles.

2. Use a pick to arrange the bangs in a way that suits the character. Use a reference picture of the character to make sure the bangs are accurate.

3. Trim the bangs. Keep in mind that wig wefts do not sit on the head the same way human hair grows from the scalp. Be sure to cut at a vertical angle, around 90°, rather than bluntly across. This will thin the wig at the ends and prevent unevenness with movement.

4. (Optional) To keep the bangs in place, lightly hairspray them after putting on the wig. This will prevent them from moving too much throughout the day.

TUTORIAL

ADDING VOLUME

While it may be time consuming, adding volume to your wig will make it stand out. It can also be an important first step to creating more dramatic styles.

Remember that heat styling will permanently change the shape of the wig, and therefore is far more reliable for styling than hairspray alone. Using the crimping method to add volume is essentially warping the fibers for easier styling.

WHAT YOU WILL NEED

Comb with a pick

Hairspray

Hair crimper

Detangling brush (optional)

Wig styling head

Steamer (optional)

Silicone-based detangling spray

1. Using your pick, separate your wig into sections. For really dramatic volume, separate into smaller sections. Always start on the bottom layers.

2. Gently back-comb the section. It will look tangled, but trust the process.

3. Spray the section on both sides with a small amount of hairspray.

4. Crimp the section at a 45° angle. Crimp again going in the opposite direction. This is to minimize crimp marks in the wig. Allow the wig to cool before the next step.

5. Brush or comb through the whole section, detangling the teasing you created in step 2. This is easier with a detangling brush, but a comb will do the trick. The result of this step might be shocking, but extreme volume is exactly what we want. If the wig has too much volume, you can use a steamer and a brush to reduce the volume at the end.

6. Repeat steps 2–5 on any other sections where you desire more volume. This could be the entire wig or just the bangs; it all depends on the look you're going for!

7. Steaming the wig is optional, but can help with creating a smoother finish. After detangling the wig, use the steamer to smooth out any sections that might have too much volume or tangles. Do this by briefly holding the steamer underneath the wig, then brushing it out.

8. If you're styling a long wig, spray the entire wig down with a detangler. Finish with a generous amount of hairspray and voila!

TUTORIAL

CURLING WIGS

Our favorite method for curling synthetic wigs is by using a steamer. Discovering this method was a game changer. For larger, more voluminous curls, you may want to first follow the Adding Volume tutorial (page 29) before proceeding with curls.

WHAT YOU WILL NEED

Wig styling head

Comb with a pick

Bobby pins, rollers, or long clips

Steamer

Hairspray

1. Place your wig on the wig styling head. Pin the hair by section into the desired curl shape using bobby pins, rollers, or long clips as follows. For the bobby pin or long clip method, wrap a section of hair around your finger until you reach the roots. Position the bobby pin around the curl at the base to secure it. For the roller method, wrap a section of hair around the rounded foam on the roller and use the roller's clip to hold it in place.

2. Use a steamer on the strands that are held in place. The wet heat will warp the fibers into the curl shape.

3. Allow the wig to air-dry with the pins, rollers, or long clips still in place. Avoid trying to speed up the process with a hair dryer, as this could cause flyaway hairs on the curl.

4. Remove the bobby pins, rollers, or long clips. Spray hairspray all over the wig to ensure the curls hold. Use a hairdryer to set the curls in place.

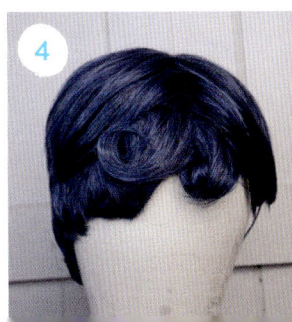

TUTORIAL

CREATING A FORMED SPIKE ON A WIG

Some characters, especially those in anime or video games, have large cartoonish spikes as an essential part of their design. Characters like Sora from *Kingdom Hearts* or Yugi from *Yu-Gi-Oh!* have hairstyles that defy gravity. With practice and patience, you can create these challenging styles at home!

WHAT YOU WILL NEED

Wig styling head

Comb with a pick

Hairspray

Hair crimper

Steamer

Scissors

Cup of water

Hair dryer

Creating cartoonish spikes to be placed in your wigs might feel very intimidating. If you understand the basics of wig styling, as we've been discussing this chapter, it won't seem as difficult! In order to create a formed spike, one must understand the tutorials on Trimming Bangs to Suit Your Face (page 26) and Adding Volume (page 29). If you are adding short spikes into long hair, make sure to shorten the hair section *before* adding volume to the spike. It will save you time later.

1. Separate the section of hair you want spiked.

(continued)

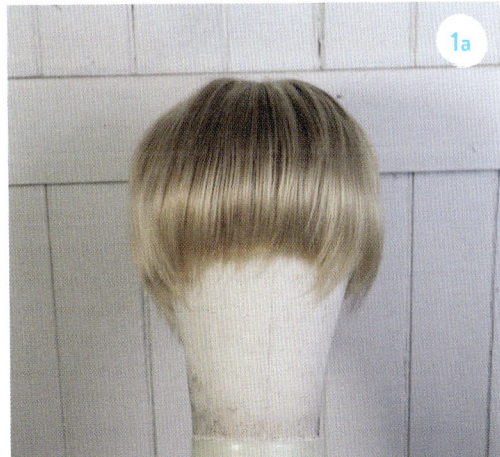
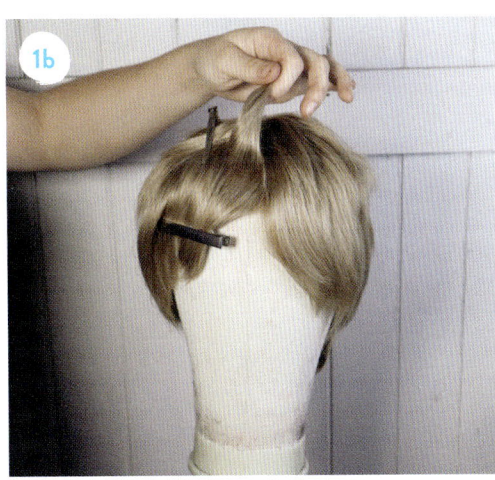

CREATING A FORMED SPIKE ON A WIG (CONTINUED)

2. Tease the wig fibers. Do this by combing backward on the hair section to tangle it, as shown in image 2b. The tighter these teased sections are, the more volume you will have after detangling. For spikes, we recommend getting as much volume as possible.

3. Use hairspray and crimp the spike.

4. Brush out the section. It should have a lot of extreme volume. This is important for the size and shape of the spike. If you aren't satisfied with the volume, repeat the steps as shown above until you achieve the desired result. The bigger the volume, the better for the next steps.

5. Turn on the steamer. Use your hands to shape the spike into the desired shape while using the steamer to apply heat. Wig fibers are best held in shape by heat warping, not just hairspray.

6. Holding the scissors at a 30° angle, cut the ends of the spike to thin it out to the required length.

7. Lightly spray the spike with hairspray. Dip your fingers in water; this will keep your hand from sticking to the wig fibers. Use that hand to refine the shape of the spike. Trim as necessary. To make the spike point, spray some hairspray directly onto your fingers and make a twisting motion on the end of the spike.

8. Generously spray the spike with hairspray. Use a hairdryer on the lowest air setting to set the spike. The hairdryer will ensure the hairspray sets completely.

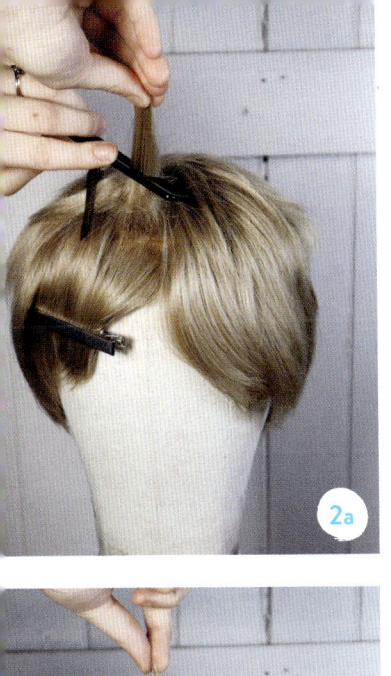

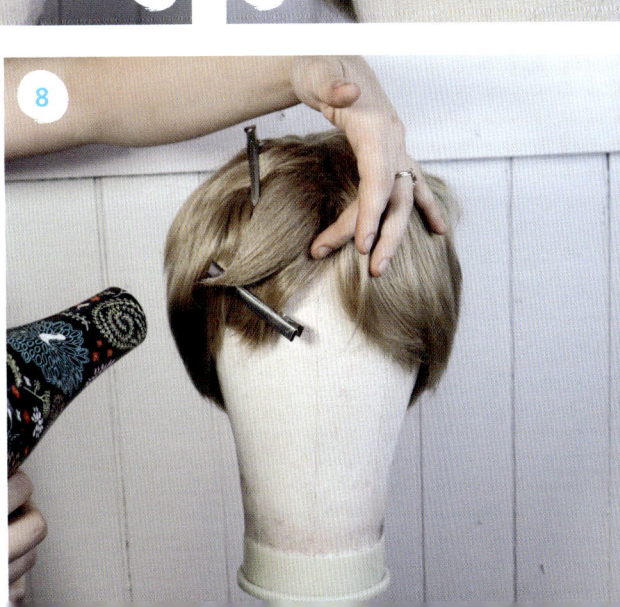

2a

2b

3

4

5

6

TUTORIAL

DYEING A WIG

Dyeing a wig is not often necessary if you buy the wig in the correct color, but sometimes it is needed, especially for ombré-colored wigs. You cannot lighten a wig with dye, but you can darken it. If you plan on dyeing a wig, starting with a light base will give you the best result. Keep color theory in mind when dyeing wigs. Unless you are starting with white, the base color will impact the final color of the wig. For example, putting blue dye on a red wig might make the wig turn out purple.

Never try to dye a wig that isn't heat resistant. If a wig isn't heat resistant, the dyeing process could ruin it. Cheaper wigs might also be made from synthetic fibers that don't respond to dye. Never attempt to fully dye a lace front wig. The fabric will dye the lace, ruining the "natural" hairline effect lace fronts are supposed to provide.

WHAT YOU WILL NEED:

Kitchen pot (do not use this pot for cooking after this project)

Synthetic fabric dye (we recommend Rit brand)

Tongs

1. Fill a large pot with water and bring to a boil.

2. Mix in the desired amount of dye. If you can't find the correct shade of fabric dye, you can custom mix your own. I highly recommend testing custom color mixes on a few strands before dyeing the full wig.

3. Submerge only the parts of the wig you want dyed. For an all-around color change, submerge the entire wig and stir with the tongs. For an ombré effect, see the tutorial for dyeing ombré fabric on page 102; it is the same process.

4. Stir the wig around until it reaches the desired shade. For pastel wigs, the wig might only need to be submerged for a few seconds. For darker wigs, the process might take a few minutes. Remember, you can always darken the wig, but you cannot lighten it once it is colored. I recommend pulling the wig out every few seconds to check the color.

5. Rinse the wig in cold water. Hot water will not set the dye. If the wig is still not dark enough, repeat the dye process.

6. Let the wig air-dry overnight. It's now ready to style!

WIG MAINTENANCE AND STORAGE

Storing wigs properly is important! If you don't store long wigs properly, it could take hours to detangle them again in the future. If you have shaped spikes on a wig, you don't want to ruin your hard work. For wigs that don't have heavy styling, it's best to store them in the bags they were shipped in. Heavily spiked wigs should be kept on a Styrofoam wig head.

You might have to clean your wig if you wear it often enough. If you get too much hairspray on the wig, too much glue, or any other grime, you know it's time for a wash. Hygiene is important when cosplaying, especially at cons. There are multiple soaps you can use to properly clean a wig. Our preferred products are either dish soap or any synthetic wig shampoo. Wash the wig in cold water and let it air-dry. If you wash the wig in hot water, it might warp the fibers of the wig.

Sometimes wigs with heavy spikes can't be washed. To sanitize wigs without washing them, fill a spray bottle with rubbing alcohol and spray it on all areas of the wig, including the inside. Let it air-dry and it will be ready to wear again.

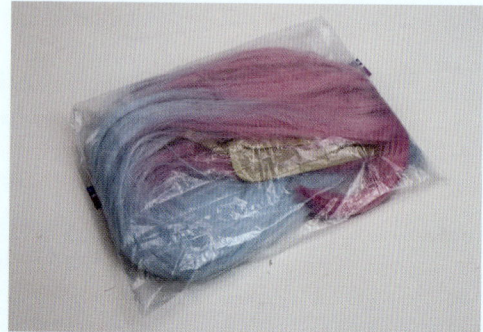

Wig in a bag

Wig on a head

Cleaning a wig >

PAINTING YOUR FACE!

Makeup is a valuable tool that can elevate your cosplays to the next level. Makeup transcends gender norms, and working with it is a skill that can bring confidence to anyone, regardless of their gender presentation in or out of cosplay. Even if the character you cosplay doesn't appear to be wearing makeup, a simple understanding of basic looks can greatly affect a finished cosplay look.

When first learning about cosplay makeup, it's vital that you understand what kind of look you are going for. Is it feminine or masculine? Are you attempting a drag-inspired approach? What are your inspirations?

The world of makeup can seem intimidating when coming in with zero to little knowledge. Even experienced makeup artists are trying new skills and products every day. The purpose of this chapter is not to tell you the perfect way to apply all makeup. It's to provide a solid foundation of various techniques applicable to cosplay.

STUDY YOUR FEATURES

It is crucial to understand your own facial features before applying makeup. Everyone has their own unique features and characteristics: the contours of your face, the shape of your eyes, your skin tone, etc. Take note of these features, especially your cheekbones, your eye shape, and your natural jawline. If you are new to doing makeup, it will take some trial and error to find a personal style that is perfect for you. It took us *years* before we were finally comfortable doing makeup on ourselves.

WHAT PRODUCTS DO YOU NEED?

There are endless makeup products on the market for almost any use imaginable. What should cosplayers carry in their makeup bag? Let's examine the products that are most effective in our makeup kit for everyday use. As a cosplayer, you might find yourself using most of these makeup supplies every time you get into cosplay!

This does not include any supplies for SFX makeup or body paint. If you are someone who wears body paint, face paint, or any other SFX makeup, it might be worthwhile to check out page 80 for what else you can add to your makeup kit.

Face primer: Regardless of brand, there are two different kinds of makeup primer and foundation: water-activated and silicone-based. If you are using water-activated primer, make sure you are not using a silicone-based foundation or your foundation will not stick on your face. Check the ingredients in your makeup before applying. Ingredients like dimethicone and cyclopentasiloxane mean a foundation is silicone-based. Research the ingredients of your makeup if you're unsure.

Eye primer: Eye primer's primary job is to provide a smooth surface for eyeshadow to seamlessly blend. It also can help eyeshadow last longer without creasing.

Foundation: Foundation is exactly what the name says, a strong foundation for the rest of your makeup. It might be worth having your skin tone properly matched at an in-person store if you are new to makeup.

BB cream: BB cream is a tinted moisturizer that can color correct and protect the skin from UV rays. For those with sensitive skin, BB cream is a low-coverage replacement option for foundation.

Cream contour: Cream contour blends into foundation a lot easier than powder contour. Cream contour palettes have a variety of shades.

Powder contour: Powder contour can be great for more natural-looking contour. Start small and build up to avoid the makeup looking patchy.

Cream blush: Cream blush is highly pigmented and blends like a dream. Some people even use cream blush as a lip tint!

Powder blush: Powder blush can be used on any part of the face and can be extremely affordable depending on the brand!

Cream bronzer: Cream bronzer can be used around the edges of the face to add dimension. It's warmer toned than cream contour and can provide a sun-kissed look.

Powder bronzer: Powder bronzer and cream bronzer are very similar in their use.

Concealer: Concealer comes in many different shades, including green and orange! Some people use concealer for color correcting. If you plan on using concealer for contouring the face, it's best to buy a concealer that is slightly lighter than your foundation shade to give your makeup a three-dimensional look!

Powder eyeshadow: There are endless possibilities when it comes to eyeshadow brands. When looking for a good eyeshadow, make sure the product blends seamlessly. Not all eyeshadows are made the same. Some eyeshadow brands are great for matte colors but terrible for shimmery shades. Test different brands to find your favorites!

Loose powder eyeshadow: Some of the best shimmer shades come in loose powder! Loose powder can be messy so be careful when handling and don't spill it.

Highlighter: Highlighter can come in liquid or liquid form. It's usually very sparkly and a little goes a long way. It's used to brighten the higher parts of the face for a dramatic glowing look. In a pinch, you can use sparkly light eyeshadow in its place!

Eyeliner: Whether your eyeliner is liquid, gel, felt tip, or pencil, all eyeliners have similar uses. Most cosplayers use a combination of brush tip or felt tip liners.

False lashes: False lashes are extremely accessible. You can even get decent quality false lashes at places like the Dollar Tree!

Lash glue: While it's easy to find decent quality lashes for cheap, the same does not apply for lash glue. DUO® has affordable lash glue and can be purchased from most drug stores!

Setting powder: Setting powder is a powder makeup created to reduce shine and creases in makeup, and it is essential to making base makeup last all day. Setting powder comes in many shades, the most popular being translucent. Don't confuse setting powder with powder foundation!

Setting spray: Setting spray is a glue-like spray intended to hold your makeup in place for long periods of time. There are many brands to try, including the extremely popular Morphe Continuous Setting Mist. If you don't have setting spray, an old drag queen trick is to use hairspray on your face instead! Be careful doing this. If you have sensitive skin this could cause major irritation.

Makeup brushes: There are tons of different kinds of makeup brushes. For cosplay, I find it only necessary to have the essentials. Small, angled brushes are very versatile for eye makeup. Large foundation brushes can be helpful to blend face makeup. Medium blush and bronzer brushes will always be used when preparing base makeup. Be sure you have enough clean brushes in your makeup kit to make the process easier.

GETTING YOUR FACE READY FOR MAKEUP

Makeup is a very artistic process. There are many amazing ways to experiment and express yourself, but preparing and protecting your skin is an important first step in the process. Proper skin prep and primer can make or break a makeup look. There are plenty of makeup brands on the market that claim to have the best products. But all you need to do is remember some basic tips and you can create an amazing cosplay makeup routine.

Before putting any makeup on your face, it's important to prepare the skin for the application. Start by washing your face and hands. Any oil or dirt on your skin will be trapped underneath the makeup you apply, which can cause irritation and breakouts and prevent your makeup from sticking to your skin. A gentle cleanser will get the job done.

Once your skin is clean, it's time to lay a base for your makeup. I always use an SPF moisturizer before putting on primer to keep the freshly washed skin healthy. Drug store brands like Olay or Cetaphil are quick and affordable.

Once the skin is protected, it's best to use a makeup primer before applying foundation or body paint. Makeup primer helps smooth out porous skin and keep makeup evenly applied on the face throughout the day.

My personal favorite foundation primer is e.l.f. Cosmetics Power Grip Primer.

It is a silicone-based primer, so I pair it with either KVD Beauty Good Apple Serum Foundation or Tarte™ Face Tape™ Foundation.

Drugstore brands like Maybelline™ and CoverGirl also have affordable silicone-based foundations. Make sure to get a foundation that matches your skin tone.

If you are using body paint (page 80), make sure you use the above tips before applying the body paint. Never use silicone-based primers with water-activated body paint. Most cream body paints are silicone-based.

FOUNDATION TECHNIQUES

For everyday makeup, a lot of people prefer to do a light foundation base. For cosplay, I usually apply foundation heavily to get maximum coverage. There are endless online hacks for applying foundation; you can even use your hands! Most makeup artists either use a foundation brush or a beauty blender.

When applying foundation, it's always better to start with less and build from there. Never apply too much all at once. Pay special attention to blending the foundation in areas like the neck, the jaw, and the sides of your nostrils.

Foundation brush: Brushes are super easy to use. Apply the foundation directly to your face and carefully spread around with your brush. Continue until the foundation blends seamlessly with your skin.

Beauty blender: The trick to beauty blenders is to get them wet before using them. It might seem odd applying makeup onto your face with a wet sponge, but this is to prevent the sponge from absorbing half of your product. Beauty blenders can be used to get a very smooth base with minimal experience, but you will usually lose a little bit of your foundation into your sponge.

Tip: Having a hard time blending heavy foundations? Try an airbrush foundation!

BASIC MAKEUP TECHNIQUES

Using makeup to shape and enhance your features is an essential part of the makeup process. Proper use of contouring techniques can help define your jawline, brighten your eyes, and create a balanced look overall. When contouring the face, it's important to choose a makeup style that best suits yourself and the character. Though makeup does not have a gender, I often refer to the two most common makeup styles as feminine and masculine. Most makeup will follow similar steps, but shape, color, and intensity can vary.

FEMININE MAKEUP

Contouring the face is done after putting on foundation to draw one's eyes to the higher points in the face. For feminine makeup, it's often used to soften the features and brighten the eyes.

For most natural feminine makeup styles, I follow these contour guidelines:

1. Using cream contour and a brush, apply contour directly underneath the jawline from ear to ear. Blend using a contour brush. Use a handheld mirror to avoid missing spots.

2. Contour the cheekbones. Starting from the edge of the face, lightly drag your contour brush/stick diagonally toward the mouth, stopping in the center of the cheek. Blend downward and out into the hairline.

3. Using a small brush, gently contour the nose. Always start small and build up to avoid the makeup looking too muddy. Blend.

4. Using a concealer lighter than your natural skin tone, apply concealer under the eyes, along the forehead, on the bridge of the nose, and on the center of the chin.

5. Let the concealer sit for ten seconds, then blend outward. The direction you blend your concealer will affect your face shape. Make sure to thoroughly blend the undereye into your waterline before blending outward toward the hairline. The goal is for the makeup to look as natural as possible.

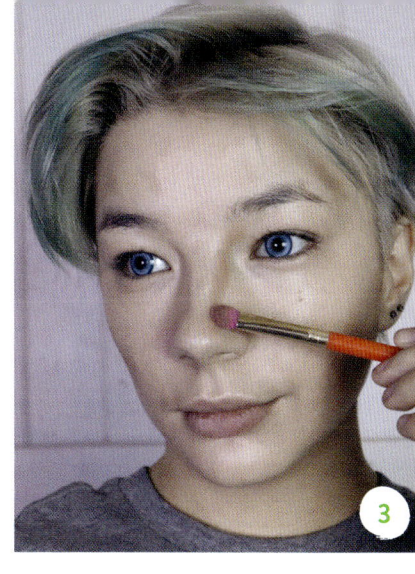
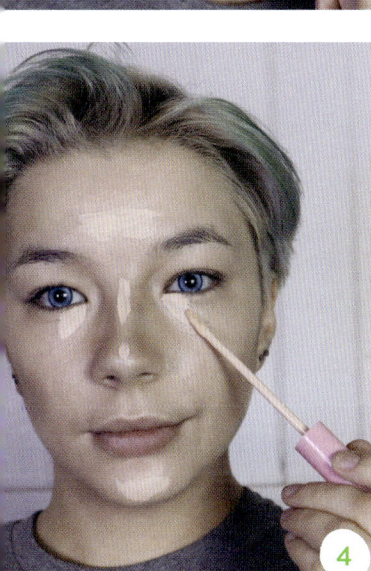

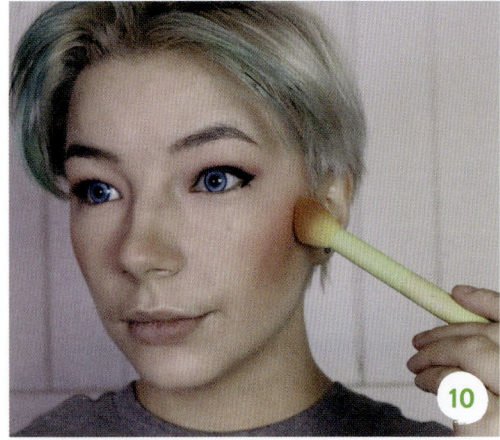

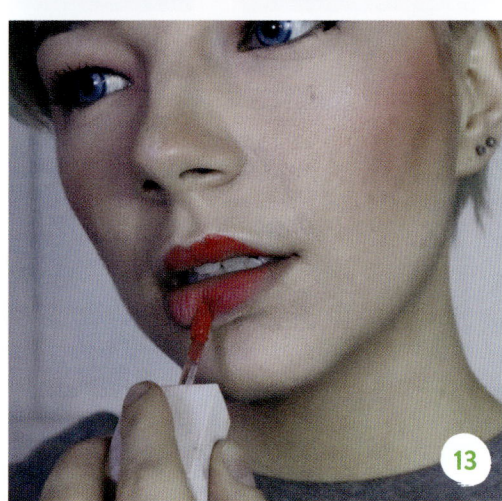

6. Set your makeup with your favorite setting powder. Gently dab the corner of a triangle powder puff into the setting powder and tap off the excess. Place the puff firmly onto your skin anywhere you have applied concealer. This will reduce creasing and shine.

7. Define your brows using eyeshadow, pomade, or pencil. Start at the inner corners and follow your brows' natural shape with light strokes. If your brows are unruly, try setting them with a clear brow gel!

8. Apply eyeshadow that complements the character's color palette. For most feminine makeup looks, I often choose a blend of natural browns and pinks to create a soft look.

- Using a medium eyeshadow brush, apply a light neutral color directly onto the entire lid. Blend outward toward the eyebrows.

- Take a darker complementary color and apply it to the outer corner, blending upward and in toward the middle of the eye.
- (Optional) Using your finger, apply a neutral glitter eyeshadow along the inner corner to make the eyes pop.

9. Apply eyeliner. Most people prefer black liquid liner, but if you're truly going for a natural look, try using brown!

- Apply a thin line on the upper lash line, being very careful to avoid applying too much product to the inner corner.
- Once you reach the outer corner, make a small wing following your natural eye shape. Fill in the wing to connect with your upper lash line.
- (Optional) Draw on a few small bottom lashes to give a slight doll-eyed look.
- (Optional) Using a white pencil eyeliner, fill in the lash line to emphasize a rounder eye.

10. Apply bronzer and blush to enhance your desired features. Not all characters need both bronzer and blush, but I find for most it gives them a touch of color that truly makes them feel three dimensional.

- For feminine characters, I always prefer to use a bronzer with a slight shimmer. Using a bronzer brush, apply bronzer in a tapping motion starting from the center of the cheekbone. Blend downward and toward the hairline. If your hairline is going to be visible, apply bronzer along the forehead the same way you applied contour. Always start small and build up to avoid looking muddy.
- Choose a blush shade that complements the character you're cosplaying. Using a blush brush, gently dust the blush directly on the cheekbones, blending up and toward the hairline. If you're using bronzer, blend the two together where the products meet. For a cuter look, apply a small amount of blush to the tip of the nose and the end of the chin. Always start small and build up.

11. Brighten the desired parts of the face using highlighter. For natural looks, it's best to use a highlighter brush as this will create a natural shimmery highlight. Tap your brush into powder highlight and gently brush over your cheekbones, just above where your blush or bronzer rests. Apply more highlighter to the bridge of the nose and directly underneath the eyebrow. Masculine characters typically have deeper-set eyes; by highlighting under the brow, you can more easily distinguish feminine-styled characters.

12. Apply your mascara by tilting your head back and holding the wand parallel to the lash line. Carefully brush the mascara from the base of your lashes to the tips. You can go over it again to get rid of any clumps. If you choose to curl your lashes with a curler, do this before applying mascara. If you choose to apply mascara to your bottom lash line, do so very carefully as the lashes are much thinner there. Make sure the mascara is completely dry before setting your makeup to avoid the mascara bleeding onto the skin. If you want to apply false lashes, now is the time (page 68).

13. There are countless ways to apply lipstick. For more natural looks, I try to choose a neutral pink color. There are three types of lipstick I choose from when doing natural makeup looks.

- **Neutral matte lipstick:** You only need one product for this: a long-lasting matte liquid lipstick. Matte liquid lipstick lasts for a long time and is harder to transfer. Using the tip of the lipstick or an angled brush, carefully trace the edges of your lip line and fill in the center. Allow to dry completely.

- **Ombré blended lip:** Some douyin or dolly styles use techniques like this. Almost any product will work. Simply take your desired lip color and gently tap it on the center of your upper and lower lip. Use your finger to blend this out. Once you're done, apply a clear lip gloss on top.

- **Full gloss lip:** My favorite style of lipstick. Try to avoid using liquid lipstick when attempting a gloss lip, as this can be very messy. Start with a lip liner and trace along your lip line to lock the color in. Fill in the center with regular lipstick of choice. Use any gloss on top for a glamorous look.

14. You're almost done! Time to set the makeup with setting spray to lock it in and hold it in place all day. Hold your setting spray 6 inches (15 cm) from your face, close your eyes, and spray evenly across your face and neck. Once it's dry, your makeup is complete!

MASCULINE MAKEUP

Masculine makeup is intended to sharpen the features and add shadows to certain parts of the face. Even a small amount of masculine face shaping can greatly improve a cosplay's quality. Basic masculine makeup takes just a few steps:

1. Apply a base of foundation or BB cream (page 46).

2. Using a contour brush, apply medium contour underneath the eyebrows, the cheekbones, the jawline, and the cupids bow as shown above. Blend.

3. Use a brow pencil to fill in your natural brows. Start from the inner brow and work outward. If your brows are thin, thicken them using feathered motions.

4. (Optional) Use a small flat brush to add a small amount of eyeshadow around the eyes. I use a combination of light brown and light purple to give a defined but natural look.

5. Set your makeup with setting spray and you're done!

Coloring Your Beard

If you're someone who can grow facial hair, it can be really fun to incorporate your beard into your cosplay. You don't need to limit yourself to characters that have hair color that matches your own. With makeup, you can change your beard color to match the character! We'll cover some of the various methods you can use to change your beard color. None of these options are permanent, so you can simply wash the color out when you're done cosplaying.

Hair wax: This is a colorful wax that you can use to coat your beard. If you want the color to be vivid, I recommend getting both white and the final color you're aiming for. Hair wax is great if you have a larger beard because the wax can be purchased cheaply in large quantities.

Eyeshadow: Eyeshadow doesn't cover hair well enough for dramatic color changes. However, it can be helpful for adding more shading and dimension.

Cream body paint: Cream body paint works better on hair than water-activated body paint, but it still wants to stick to skin more than hair follicles. For this reason, I don't recommend using it unless you don't have other options.

Eyebrow pomade: Eyebrow pomade comes in small containers but is highly pigmented. A little bit goes a long way. This product is great if you have a shorter beard.

TUTORIAL

CHANGING THE COLOR OF A LONG BEARD

If you are an individual with the dedication to grow out a long beard, you will probably be hesitant to shave it off for a cosplay. Instead, you might be inclined to change the color of your beard to suit whichever character you choose!

WHAT YOU NEED

Gloves

Hair wax in white and final color

Hairdryer (optional)

Eyeshadow in shades of final color and a makeup brush (optional)

1. Put on your gloves and scoop up some of the white hair wax.

2. Massage the white hair wax into your beard using your fingers, being careful to avoid your skin.

3. Once your beard is fully white, let it dry for 10–15 minutes. You can also use a hairdryer to speed up the process.

4. Repeat the process with the colorful hair wax, fully covering your beard.

5. (Optional) Use eyeshadow in your final color to add more depth and colors onto your beard. You'll need to use a large amount of powder to make an impact.

TUTORIAL

CHANGING THE COLOR OF A SHORT OR SPARSE BEARD

If you are able to grow out stubble or short facial hair, it is possible to change the color. This might suit someone more than purchasing fake facial hair or drawing illusion makeup directly onto the skin. Shave your facial hair evenly before attempting this!

WHAT YOU NEED

Spoolie brush

Eyebrow pomade in your final color

Eyeshadow in shades of your final color

Flat angled makeup brush

Setting spray

1. Rub the spoolie brush in the eyebrow pomade. Use the spoolie to apply pomade to your beard. Take care to only cover the hair follicles and not your skin.

2. Using eyeshadow, simulate hair follicles with small, short strokes of your flat angled makeup brush in the empty patches of your beard. Mixing in a variety of shades can make your beard look more realistic.

3. When you're happy with the result, spray with a setting spray to fully set the makeup.

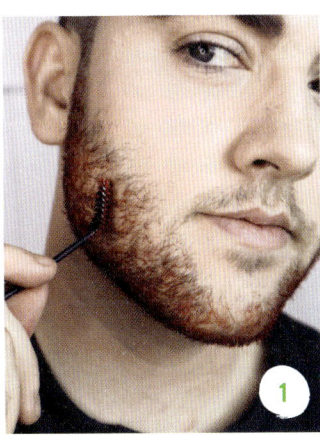  

TUTORIAL

COVERING A BEARD

For someone who can grow facial hair, shaving won't be enough to fully hide the traces of a beard. The area where your beard used to be will still have a cooler tone compared to the rest of your skin. Even if you use full coverage foundation, the difference in the undertones will hint at where your facial hair used to be. Fortunately, makeup can solve this!

What shade and color you use to color correct your beard is very specific to the individual. Someone of a darker complexion will need to use different shades than someone who has fair skin. The number of cool tones you have that need to be corrected also varies by individual. Generally speaking, if you have fair skin, color correct with a peach tone. If you have darker skin, color correct with a darker orange tone. The only way to determine the right color corrector shade for you is by experimenting and practicing yourself.

WHAT YOU WILL NEED

Primer

Orange or peach color corrector (preferably cream, not powder)

Beauty blender or makeup brush

Full coverage foundation or concealer

Translucent setting powder

1. Start with a shaved face; you'll want as close of a shave as possible. Apply your favorite primer to your entire face.

2. Now it's time to color correct the cool tones left by your beard. Apply an orange or peach toned color corrector. The exact shade and amount you use will depend on your skin's individual shade and the number of cool tones you need to correct.

3. Apply your favorite full coverage foundation or concealer over your entire face.

4. Set your makeup with a translucent setting powder.

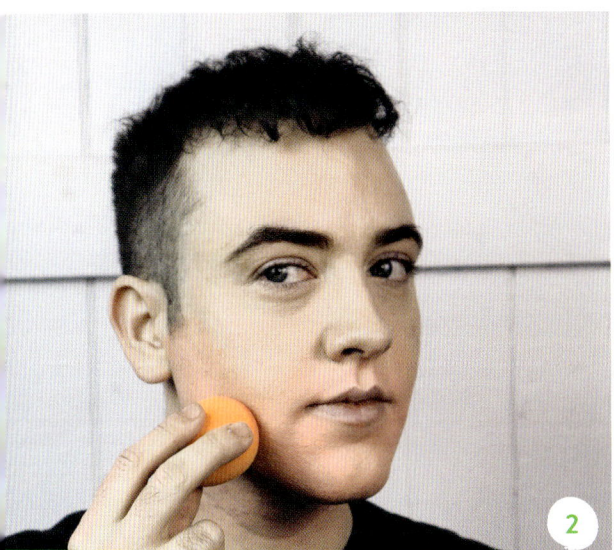

DRAG MAKEUP

What is drag and why is it included in a cosplay book? Drag is an art form involving performance, makeup, and gender expression and is a crucial part of LGBTQ+ culture. Drag artists often use makeup and acting to push the boundaries of gender roles and identity. Cosplayers and drag artists often have cultural overlap in this way.

Drag has been a huge inspiration for my own cosplay design. I often reference drag kings and queens for makeup and wig inspiration. While there are no limits to what drag makeup looks like, this guide will explain how we apply our own exaggerated makeup styles.

DRAG QUEEN

My personal favorite style of drag queen makeup is very exaggerated and angular. Large pops of color, lots of glitter, and very exaggerated feminine features are the three parts I focus on the most. Before starting, be sure you have an idea of what you want your makeup to look like.

Gluing Down Eyebrows

Before you apply your foundation, decide if your look requires you to glue down your eyebrows. This will provide extra room for exaggerated eye makeup as well as a blank slate for creating a new eyebrow shape. While there are products on the market that can be used to glue down eyebrows, the most popular method is to use a purple disappearing glue stick from the craft aisle!

(continued)

GLUING DOWN EYEBROWS (CONTINUED)

1. Wipe your eyebrows down with rubbing alcohol to remove any remaining oils or product. Allow them to dry completely.

2. Wipe the glue stick directly onto the eyebrows going in the opposite direction the eyebrows naturally grow. Start from the outer corner and work inward to fully saturate the brow.

3. Comb the glue and fully work it into the eyebrows in every direction to fully saturate the hair.

4. Comb the hair upward so that it lays flat against your forehead. Use a metal spoon to help smooth the surface. If there are any clumps of glue on the skin, use rubbing alcohol and a cotton swab to clean it up.

5. Once the glue is dry, use a beauty wedge to apply a generous amount of setting powder to the glued eyebrows, pressing firmly. Allow the setting powder to sit for 5–10 minutes.

6. Use a large makeup brush to gently dust away the excess setting powder.

7. Apply a generous amount of concealer on top of the eyebrows using a makeup wedge. Firmly press the product into the brows and blend. Allow it to dry completely. Repeat this step as needed until the brows are fully covered.

8. Use a beauty blender to fully blend the product into the skin. Now you can complete the rest of your makeup!

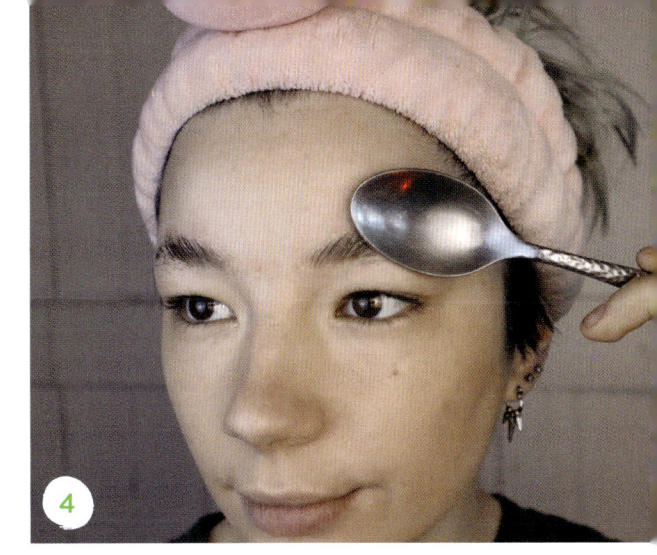

Exaggerated Eye Makeup

Dramatic eye makeup is essential for amplifying makeup and exaggerating one's features. There are endless possibilities for doing drag eye makeup. For this look we will be doing an intense pink eye look with rhinestones and bottom lashes. The steps in this tutorial can easily be translated to other colors and styles!

When applying eyeshadow with a ton of glitter, it's best to do eye makeup before your face makeup to avoid any eyeshadow falling onto existing makeup.

1. Using a white liquid or gel liner, draw a line along the inner corner of the eye to the outer corner in the desired exaggerated shape.

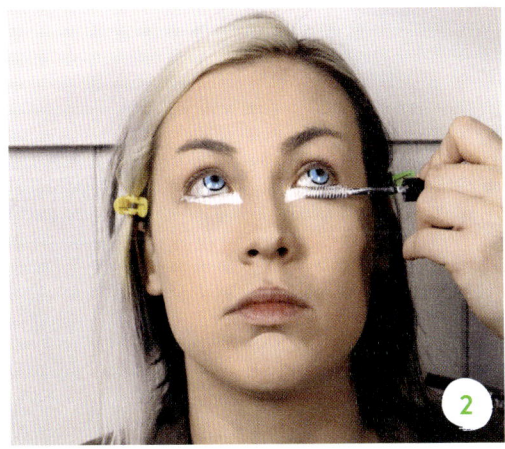

2. Once the white eyeliner is dried, apply a layer of white mascara over the bottom lashes. This will visually blend your natural lashes with the eyeliner.

3. Using a black liquid liner, draw a thin black line along your top lash line. Draw a line on the outer corner at a 45-degree angle to create a large wing. Connect the tip of the wing with your top lash line and fill in the wing with black liner until the desired wing thickness is achieved.

(continued)

PAINTING YOUR FACE!

65

4

5a

5b

5c

6a

6b

7

8

9

4. Use your black liner to draw a short black line under the white eyeliner to create a false waterline.

5. Connect the black inner corner of your natural eye to the inner corner of the white eyeliner.

6. Apply a medium purple above the top eyeliner outline, drawing a line until it meets with the edge of the outline. Blend upward and out toward the forehead and temple. Be careful when applying darker colors. Always tap the excess off before applying it to avoid using too much product and muddying the look.

7. Using a brush or your finger, take a lavender eyeshadow and blend it onto the inner eyelid lid.

8. Apply a small amount of highlighter just underneath the eyebrows. This will make the eyes pop dramatically.

9. Use black liquid liner to fix any parts of the eyeliner that might have been covered by excess eyeshadow.

10. Fill in the white eyeliner underneath the eye, fully defining its shape. Use your favorite black mascara on your top lash line. If you are not wearing false lashes, it's best to apply two to three layers.

11. If applicable, apply false lashes (see page 68).

12. To add a dramatic effect to the look, use thin white eyeliner to draw a thin line directly above the black eyeliner on the upper lid. Allow this to dry.

13. Once the eyeshadow is done, set the eye makeup with setting spray to lock in the look before continuing.

PAINTING YOUR FACE!

False Eyelashes

Some makeup techniques require a tiny bit of lash glue, whether it's for false lashes or other small details. False lashes truly add a layer of depth that two-dimensional makeup cannot achieve on its own. For drag looks, the bigger the lash the better. For this look, we're going to apply both top and bottom lashes for a more dramatic effect.

1. Take your clean lash in hand and apply a thin layer of eyelash glue along the band. Allow to dry for 15 seconds.

2. Once the lash is tacky, firmly press it onto your lash line and hold for 10 seconds. Once you let go, the lash may try to stick up at the edges. Gently adjust the lash and press down again until the lash is completely dry.

3. For the bottom lashes, cut a pair of symmetrical lashes down the center. Using small scissors, trim the center of each lash to blend seamlessly with the lash line.

4. Apply a thin layer of lash glue and allow to dry until tacky, about 15 seconds. Press firmly onto the edge of the black eyeliner you've drawn on. Hold until the lash is dried, about 10 seconds.

Gems

Gems or other similar facial accessories can draw attention to your features when attempting dramatic makeup. I've used gems to symbolize tears, freckles, and even fae jewelry. Applying gems using lash glue can be a bit tricky. If you're not careful, the gem could stick to your hand or your tweezers. The trick is applying a small amount to the face and allowing it to get tacky before attempting to stick any gems to the skin.

1. Apply a small amount of lash glue directly to the face. Allow to dry for a few seconds.

2. Press the gem directly onto the lash glue. The gem should stick on its own. Repeat for as many gems as needed.

Drag Queen Face Makeup

Eye makeup can be messy, especially if you use glitter. The fallout from the eyeshadow can ruin the lower half of your makeup, which is why so many makeup artists do eye makeup first. Once your eye makeup is complete and fully set, you can begin the rest of your facial makeup. First, prep your skin and base foundation (page 46). Then, follow this guide for contour and face shaping.

1. Using a foundation brush, draw a line of cream or powder bronzer directly underneath the cheekbone starting from the center of the cheek and ending near the hairline. Blend.

2. Apply blush directly onto the cheekbones. Blend the blush upward and toward the temples. The blush and bronzer should blend seamlessly.

3. Add a bit of concealer to the bridge of the nose and blend. Using your blush brush, dust a bit of blush around the tip of the nose.

4. It's time to draw a line to truly give the makeup that "wow" factor. Use a foundation brush and dip into your favorite foundation. Draw a line from your cheekbone to the corner of your mouth. Blend this downward to preserve the integrity of the makeup.

5. Blend the foundation into the lower half of the face, avoiding the jawline. Use setting powder and a triangle powder puff to set this layer of makeup.

6. Use your finger to apply highlighter and emphasize the brightest parts of the face. For drag looks I apply highlighter to the cheekbones, the nose bridge, the chin, and directly underneath the eyebrows.

Overlining the Lips

Drag characteristics are exaggerated and often oversized! For dramatic makeup, overlining the lips can really emphasize the features of a character. It might seem intimidating to overline your lips at first, but with practice, this style of makeup can actually be very simple!

1. Starting at the corners of your mouth, draw the outline of the lip makeup using a dark lip liner. Create your desired lip shape.

2. Fill in the lips and repeat along the bottom lip.

3. Using a darker lip liner, apply a darker shade along the edges of the lipstick. Blend this inward to make the lips appear larger.

4. Add glitter eyeshadow or lip gloss on top and the lips are finished!

 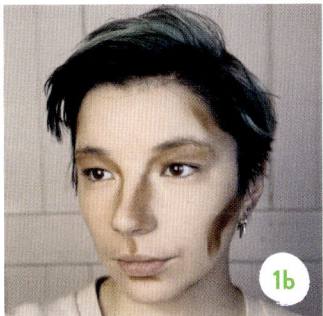 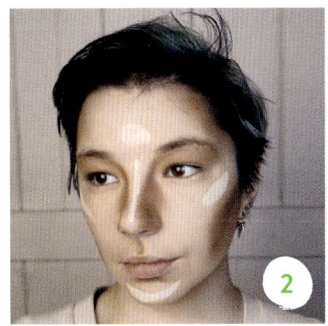
 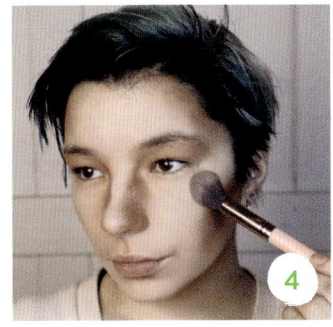 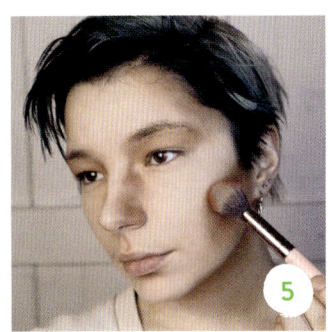

DRAG KING

Like drag queens, drag kings often have extremely exaggerated and heavily stylized makeup meant to stand out on stage. When I do drag king makeup, my goal is to use heavy contour and colors to create a caricature of the masculine character I'm cosplaying. Before starting your contour, apply primer and foundation (page 46).

Drag King Base Makeup

1. Use a dark cream contour and a foundation brush to draw dark contour lines onto the face in the following areas: underneath your natural cheekbones, your temples, underneath your brows, either side of your nose, your cupids bow, and directly above your chin underneath your lips. The contour should be applied heavier under the cheekbones and brow bone.

2. Apply concealer to the following areas: your nasal bridge, the center of your forehead above the brows, your chin, and your cheekbones.

3. Blend the concealer and contour using a blending sponge to sculpt the features of the face.

4. Set the cream makeup using a fluffy brush and setting powder.

5. Using a blush brush, apply some peachy blush to the areas with the dark contour to add some color to the face.

Drag King Eyebrows

Drag king eyebrows are bold, dramatic, and defined.

1. Mix a water-activated black graphic liner with a small amount of setting spray using a small angled brush.

2. Carefully draw an outline for your brows as desired, leaving the tops of the brows untouched.

3. Fill in the eyebrows with brown eyeshadow using careful wisping motions. Repeat this step with as many shades of brown as desired. Always start small and build up the color to avoid the brows looking muddy.

4. Set with setting spray, and the eyebrows are complete!

Fake Facial Hair

There are two ways to have fake facial hair in cosplay. You can either draw it on, or you can use prosthetics.

Drawing on Facial Hair

The trick to drawing on facial hair is to use layers of different colored eyeshadow and small feathering motions with a brush. Use a small brush and start with the lightest color to create the base shape of the facial hair. Repeat this process with darker colors until you get the desired result.

Drawing on Facial Hair

Gluing on Facial Hair

There are a lot of different places to buy fake facial hair. My personal favorite business is Act One Costumes. They're a small business that sells affordable, high-quality pieces.

There are many different types of glue to attach facial hair: Spirit gum, Bold Hold, even eyelash glue! If you want your fake facial hair to stay for a very long time, I recommend Pros-Aide®. This is a specialized prosthetic facial adhesive. Be sure to purchase the remover as well! Apply the Pros-Aide directly to the face and allow the glue to dry. Once it's tacky, firmly press the facial hair down and hold until completely dry.

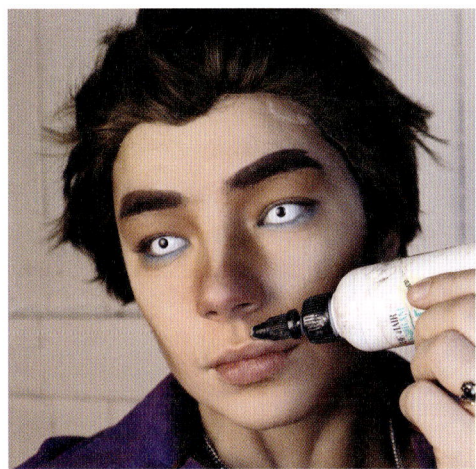

Gluing on Facial Hair Part One

Gluing on Facial Hair Part Two

PROSTHETIC BODY PIECES

Drag artists are often known for their usage of hyper realistic silicone props. We use these props often! While they are not necessary, these props can elevate drag looks.

Where to Buy

Silicone props can be expensive. Low-quality silicone pieces can be too thin, too fragile, or even a health hazard if the silicone piece was manufactured in poor conditions. We find it's worthwhile to spend the time to research the best prosthetic pieces for your own needs. A good, mid-ranged silicone piece will range upward of $250.

You can find decent quality silicone pieces of all types and sizes on Amazon. For masculine muscle suits, Smitizen has amazing quality and a huge selection. For fake breasts, Softmary has extremely high quality pieces. Keep in mind that both of these websites contain NSFW content.

How to Wear

Silicone chest prosthetics can be worn just like a T-shirt. I recommend never having them directly over skin alone, as the silicone can cause extreme sweating. I always wear a T-shirt or tank top underneath. This makes it easier to put on or take off the prosthetic. Before putting on the prosthetic, apply a generous amount of baby powder on the inside. This will make it easier to put on.

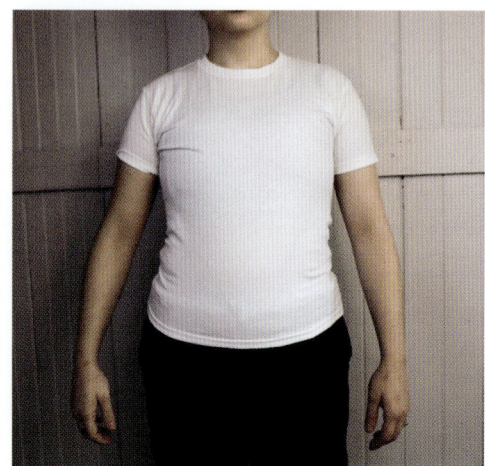

Before Muscle Suit

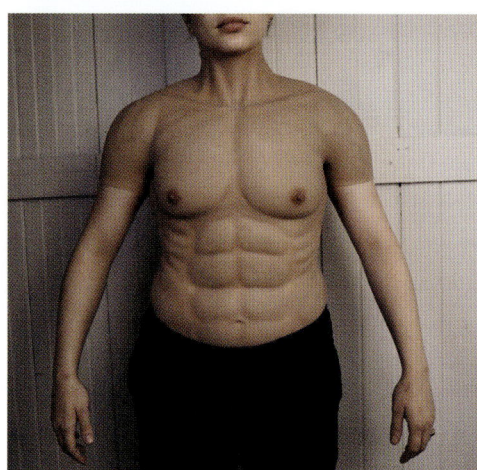

After Muscle Suit

Before Corset and Hip Pads

After Corset and Hip Pads

Corsets and Hip Pads

When I do a drag queen look, I want the silhouette of the body to have an extreme hourglass. Getting a high-quality, steel-boned waist corset is a way to do this comfortably and effectively.

Simply cinch your corset and wear hip pads on top to give yourself a snatched shape. Remember that silhouetting is all about proportions. Do not focus on cinching the waist as tight as possible. Focus instead on adding fullness to the other parts of the body.

Tip: Never double knot the ties on a corset. In an emergency, it's important to be able to unlace yourself as quickly as possible.

SFX LOOKS

BODY PAINT

Do you want to cosplay as a green orc or a red demon? Time to bust out some body paint and get colorful! Body paint can be incredibly transformative. It's great for cosplaying non-human and supernatural creatures.

Never use body paint to darken your skin color in an attempt to emulate a different race. Blackface has a long history tied to racism and dehumanization. It originated in the 19th century in minstrel shows as a way to mock and stereotype Black people. Even if mockery is not your intention, painting your skin black invokes a racist and painful history. It has no place in the cosplay community. Even when cosplaying non-humans, be mindful of how your body paint color choices could be perceived by others.

Common Types of Body Paint

We'll cover some of the body paint options most commonly used by beginners. People debate about which type is best, but often it comes down to preference. Avoid cheap kids' face paint and look for brands used by artists. This will help you get a better result, and you'll have a more enjoyable experience. The absolute most important thing is to only use products that are intended for the skin and are non-toxic. That means absolutely no Sharpies®.

Tip: If you are using body paint, make sure you use the tips on page 45 before applying the body paint. Never use silicone-based primers with water-activated body paint. Most cream body paints are silicone-based.

Water-activated: Water-activated body paint is the most common type of body paint. This paint is activated by water and it comes off with water. It is the most beginner friendly. Unfortunately, it doesn't hold up well to sweat or tears. Some brands are Ben Nye® Aqua, Fusion Body Art, Diamond FX, Mehron Paradise™ paints, or Snazaroo™ for a budget in-store option.

Grease: Grease body paint is oil-based and is set with translucent powder. It is highly pigmented and gives full coverage. It stays in place and isn't impacted by sweat or water. The downside is that it's difficult to remove and some people find it feels heavy on their skin. It is difficult to blend with other shades of grease paint. Grease paint works well for a base layer or uniform color; it is popular for clown makeup.

Cream: Cream body paint doesn't require water activation to use. It needs to be set with translucent powder like grease paint, but feels less heavy on the skin. It has more coverage than water-activated paint, but less coverage than grease. It's fairly easy to blend cream body paint. Cream paint can crack if applied too heavily.

Colored foundations: Colored foundations are a fairly new type of product. They function the same as regular foundation, except they come in vivid colors. These are lightweight and blendable, but tend to be less opaque. We found ourselves having to apply multiple layers and have had some issues with patchiness.

Liquid: Liquid body paint comes in bottles and can be applied with a sponge, brush, or airbrush. Airbrushing can have a beautiful result, but isn't beginner friendly.

Most body paint can be applied similarly to foundation. We recommend using either a makeup brush or a disposable beauty wedge to blend the body paint to avoid ruining an expensive beauty blender. Applying body paint correctly will take lots of practice, so don't be afraid of making mistakes.

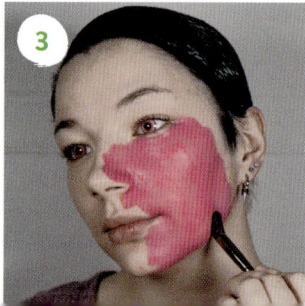
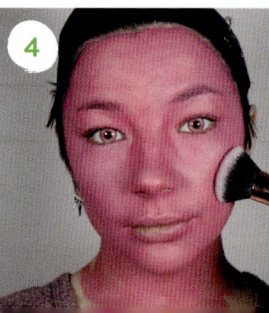

TUTORIAL

APPLYING A WATER-ACTIVATED BODY PAINT

Water-activated body paint is applied differently than foundation. It's important to get a perfect mix of water and paint for an even, full-coverage layer.

WHAT YOU WILL NEED

Foundation brush

Water

Water-activated body paint

Translucent setting powder

Beauty wedge

Setting spray

1. Wet your brush with water. Squeeze out the excess with your fingers. It's better to start with too little water than too much.

2. Mix your brush thoroughly into the paint to activate it. The goal is to create a creamy consistency. Pick up as much product as possible with the brush. If the brush is not picking up the desired amount of paint, repeat step 1 until the brush is fully saturated.

3. Apply the paint directly to the face and spread it around with the brush. The goal is to get opaque, even coverage in one layer. Trying to apply multiple layers with water-activated paint can result in patchy coverage.

4. Once the makeup is completely spread, apply a generous amount of translucent setting powder using a beauty wedge. Press the powder firmly into the face and allow it to sit for 5–10 minutes to fully set.

5. Apply an even layer of setting spray before layering on any other makeup.

TUTORIAL

AGING YOURSELF WITH MAKEUP

Typically, people try to use makeup to look younger, but you can do the opposite as well! Aging yourself with makeup can be a dramatic way to transform yourself into a character. There is no need to limit yourself to ages close to your own for cosplay.

Before you put on any makeup, examine your face. If you're old enough to have signs of aging, use those natural features to your advantage. Before adding new lines, you'll want to exaggerate the wrinkles and eyebags you already have. You may find that exaggerating these existing features is enough to get you looking older. This approach often yields a more natural look.

Even if you don't have any resting wrinkles, you may have some creases when your face is in motion. Play around with furrowing and raising your brows to get an idea of where lines on your face would naturally form. This method will customize the wrinkles you draw for your individual features. If you get very few creases even when your face is in motion, you can simply draw wrinkles where most people get them.

WHAT YOU WILL NEED

Primer

Foundation

Contour brush or makeup sponge

Contour palette with a range of light to dark shades

Eyeshadow in shades of gray, green, or blue

Two small angled makeup brushes

Brown eyeliner

Setting powder or spray

1. Gather some reference images of the intended age group and examine their faces. Having a visual of what your goal is will help you hit the target.

(continued)

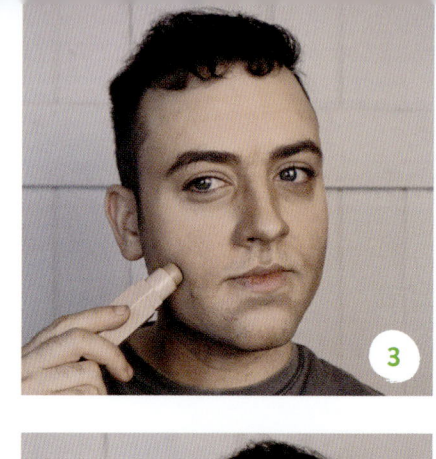
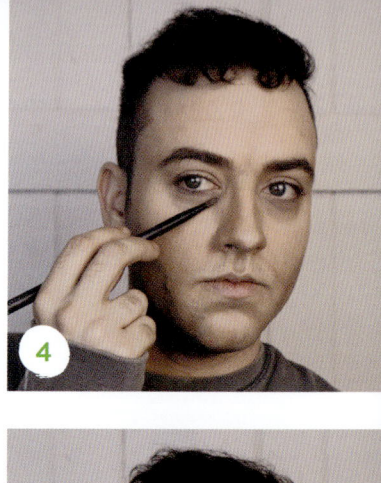

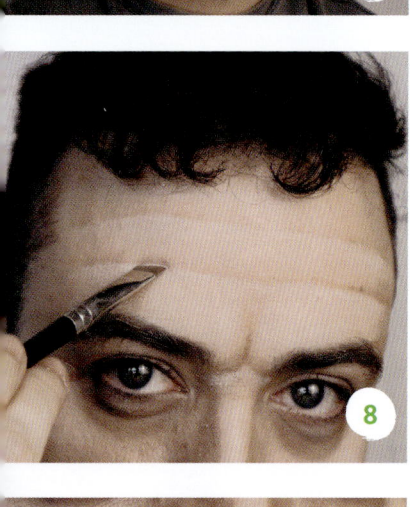
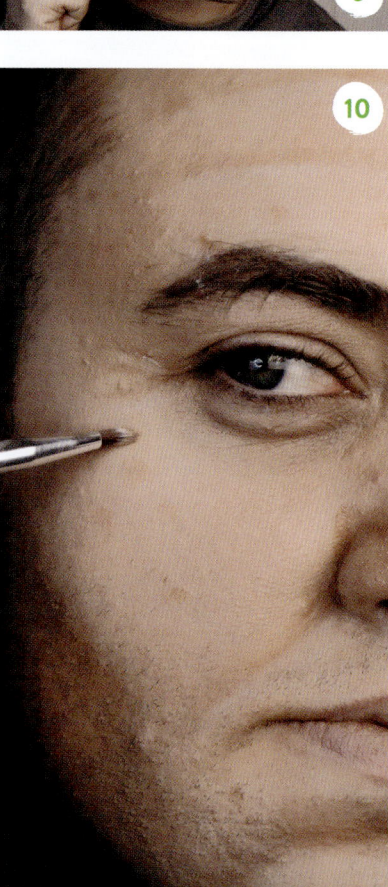
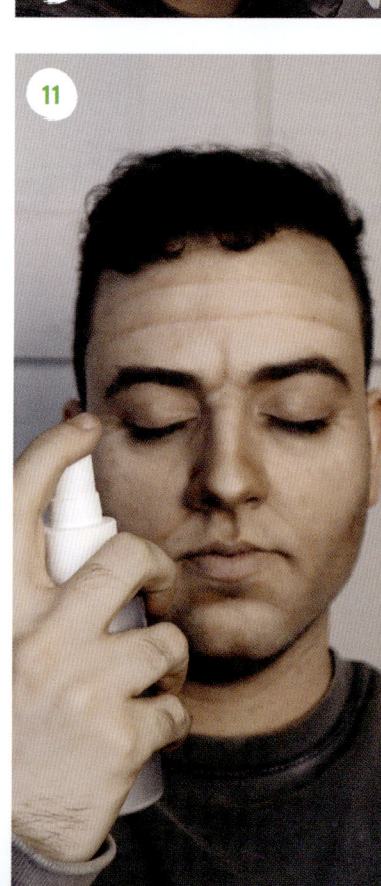

AGING YOURSELF WITH MAKEUP (CONTINUED)

2. Apply your favorite primer and your regular foundation to create a base (page 46).

3. Using a contour brush or makeup sponge, apply a medium contour shade to the hollows of your cheekbones, temples, the ridge of the chin, sides of the nose, eyebags, and philtrum. The goal is to exaggerate the creases and sunken-in areas of the face.

4. Exaggerate your eyebags with gray eyeshadow. Very small amounts of blue or green can also be used. Be careful not to go too far with this. You can end up looking sick or like you have a black eye instead of appearing old.

5. Pick a light shade of contour or concealer to highlight the areas you want to protrude outward. Focus on the cheekbones, brow ridge, the middle of the nose, chin, and the small triangle around the chin to create jowls. Add highlights to the bags of your eyes so they look puffier.

6. Pick a dark shade of contour to add more depth in the hollows that need more contrast.

7. Use the small angled makeup brush to create wrinkles. Create the wrinkles following the patterns already on your face as much as possible. A wrinkle is made from a dark line on top and a light line on bottom; the colors meet in the middle as a hard edge and are diffused outward. Start with the dark lines and blend them upward only.

8. With your second small angled makeup brush, draw the highlight directly below the dark line. Blend the light lines downward only.

9. To create wrinkles on your lips, apply a medium shade of contour or eyeshadow to your lips. Powder them with setting powder. Then pucker your lips and apply a highlight shade of contour or eyeshadow.

10. If you want to go even further, you can add brown aging spots and exaggerate the lines even more. It all depends on how aged you're trying to look!

11. Seal the look with setting spray.

TUTORIAL

SCAR MAKEUP

Scars can have a wide variety of appearances depending on how an individual heals. They can fade to a flat white line or be a raised dark red. Some scars have a variety of shades within them. Do some research to get an idea of what kind of scar you want your cosplay to have.

A great beginner-friendly product for scarring effects is rigid collodion. Rigid collodion is a clear scarring liquid that tightens and puckers the skin where it is applied. It creates texture that helps mimic the look of scarred flesh. A small bottle can be purchased online for under $10. Be sure to patch test a small area to make sure irritation doesn't occur. It's not recommended for use on sensitive skin, sensitive areas of the face, or over hair. Use rigid collodion in a well-ventilated area.

MATERIALS

Pink and fleshed tone eye shadow, lip liner, foundation, or grease paint

Rigid collodion

1. Draw on the scar. Check your scar reference image to determine which shades are appropriate. To draw on the scar you can use eyeshadow, lip liner, foundation, or even grease paint. Which type of makeup you use to draw on the scar will depend on how dramatic a scar you want. Simple flesh-toned eyeshadow works perfectly fine for a basic scar. Use multiple shades if you want a more dynamic-looking wound. The rigid collodion will dramatically change the look of the scar once it's applied so don't worry too much if it doesn't look very realistic yet.

2. Brush collodion over the scar in a thin coat. You will feel your skin tightening immediately as the collodion dries. This creates a small indentation in your skin. Wait 2–3 minutes to dry.

Tip: For deeper scar wounds, add more layers of rigid collodion. Make sure to let each layer dry before applying another.

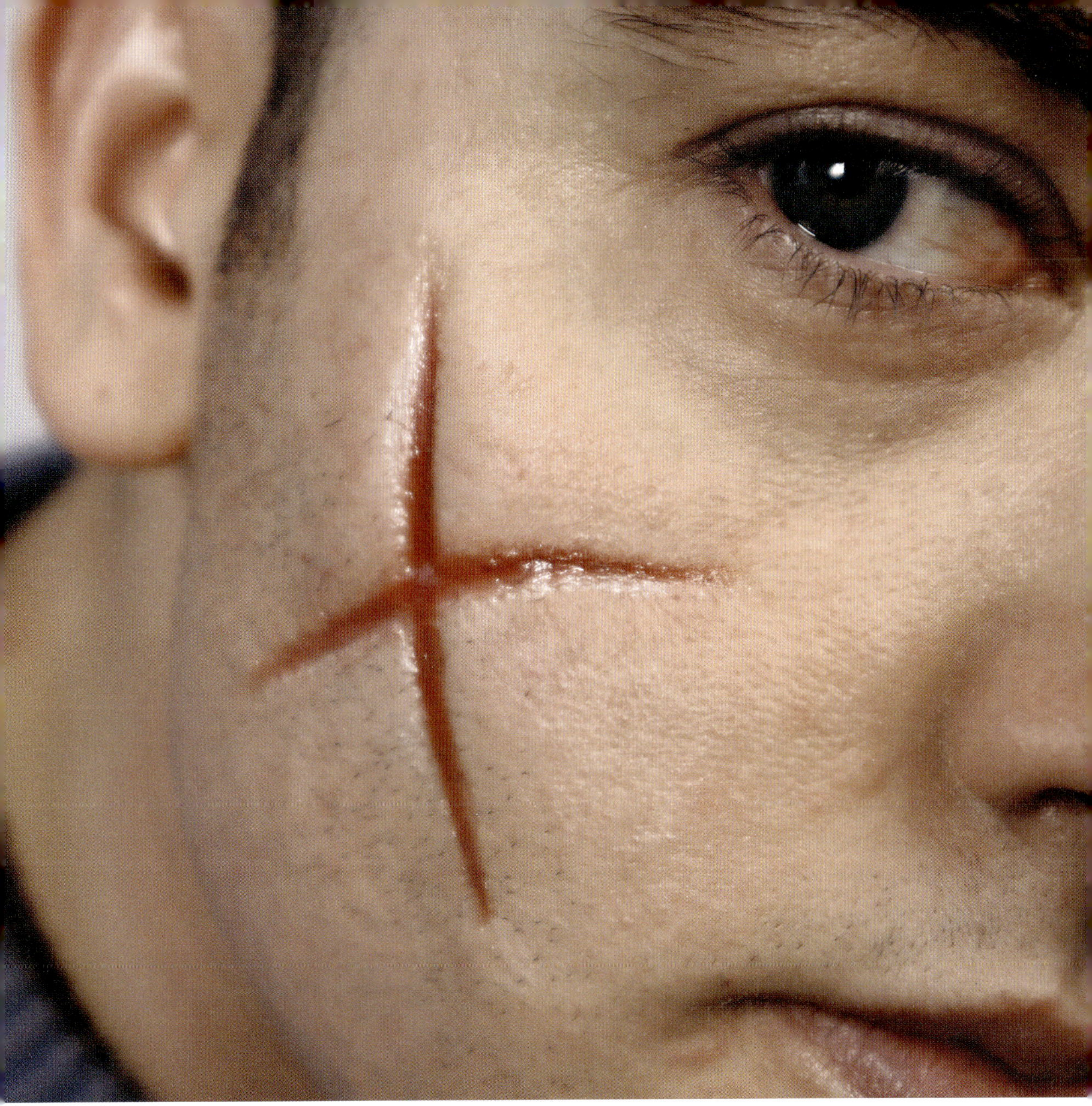

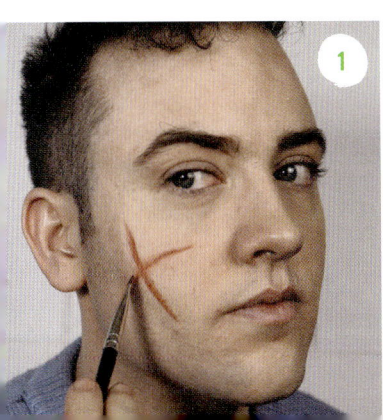

FAKE BLOOD BASICS

Alright all you aspiring vampires out there, it's the moment you've been waiting for: blood. Fake blood can help your horror cosplays stand out with eye-catching effects. If you search for fake blood you'll come up with a wide variety of options. It can be hard to know what to pick! Choosing the right type will help you get your intended effect and hopefully avoid a mess. You first need to know what type of wound or effect you're creating.

Keep in mind that pretty much all fake blood will stain fabric, especially if it's white. These stains can be difficult to get out. Not all fake blood is safe for consumption. Make sure to check that your fake blood is edible before putting any in your mouth.

Blood Color

The color of blood can quickly communicate the age of the blood and the origin of the wound.

Bright red blood: Arterial blood is oxygenated blood that flows through the arteries. It's bright red in color. It's good for fresh wounds.

Dark blood: Venous blood is dark red in color and flows through the veins. Blood of darker shades is good for deep wounds or somewhat aged blood.

Brown blood: Aged blood will turn brown or rusty in color when it has dried and aged.

Textures

Liquid stage blood: This typically comes in jugs or bottles. It's a runny liquid that you can buy in various shades. Liquid stage blood is great for staining clothes or props. Because it is very runny and it tends to stain skin very easily, we don't recommend using this product directly on the skin.

Gel blood: This is sometimes referred to as thickened blood, scab blood, or coagulated blood. It's thick in texture like jelly. It's great for adding texture to wounds.

Spray blood: This is the same as liquid blood except it's purchased in a spray bottle. It's very runny and great for creating splatter effects. It can get messy easily.

Eye blood: This blood is specially formulated so it can be applied directly to the eye using a dropper. It creates a spooky crying-blood effect which can be dramatic for videos. You can't use it with contacts.

Blood capsules: After you bite a capsule, the blood powder colors your saliva, which results in a realistic blood effect. The capsule can be hidden in your mouth and activated at will. They're useful for making videos.

TUTORIAL

GHOST MAKEUP

In this tutorial, I'll walk you through the steps to create a simple ghostly makeup look. Feel free to take inspiration, experiment, and create your own unique look!

WHAT YOU WILL NEED

Sponge, beauty blender, or large flat makeup brush

White body paint (such as Mehron Clown White and Ben Nye white creme color)

White or translucent setting powder

Gray body paint (such as Ben Nye grey creme color)

Small makeup brush for details

Black lipstick

Light gray lipstick

Eyeshadow palette with shades of gray

Black eyeliner

White eyeliner

White mascara

White eyebrow pomade and spoolie brush (optional)

1. Start with a clean face. If you plan on wearing contacts, many people prefer to put them on before their body paint. People with long hair may want to wear a wig cap.

2. Use your sponge, beauty blender, or large flat makeup brush to apply your base layer of white paint. Sponges and beauty blenders can help you avoid making brushstroke marks, but can take longer to use. I used a small amount of Mehron Clown White to get the coverage I was looking for.

3. If you used a grease or cream body paint, set this base layer with generous amounts of setting powder.

(continued)

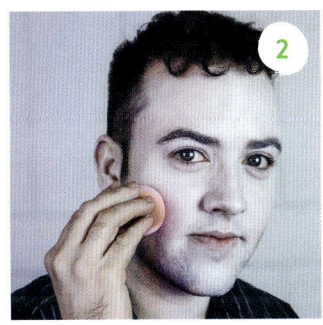 

4

5

6

7

8

9

GHOST MAKEUP (CONTINUED)

4. Contour your face with light gray body paint. Feel free to mix it with white to get various shades. Get creative here. While I'm using gray, ghosts can also be done with light greens and blues.

5. Create highlights using more white body paint on your cheek bones, jawline, chin, nose, and brow. When satisfied, set with setting powder.

6. I like to use black lipstick on my upper lip and a light gray on the bottom for a cartoonishly styled effect.

7. Use eyeshadow to add more shading to your face as needed. Add dark gray to your eyelids and below your eye. This gives the eyes a hollow, sunken look.

8. Use black eyeliner and white eyeliner to outline your eyes. Drawing extra black and white lines below the eyes creates a fun spooky effect.

9. Apply white mascara.

10. (Optional) If you're wearing a white wig, it can be fun to make your eyebrows white as well. Use a spoolie brush to apply white eyebrow pomade to your eyebrows. Add some gray shading around your eyebrows so they don't blend in with the white of your skin.

11. Seal your makeup with translucent setting powder or setting spray.

CONTACT LENS BASICS

Colored contacts can be an amazing way to make your cosplay makeup pop! If you choose to wear colored contacts with your cosplay, it is vital you understand the basics of contact safety to avoid damaging your eyes. Never feel pressured to wear contacts for cosplay if it's not something you're comfortable with. Before wearing colored contacts, visit an eye care professional to make sure that colored contacts are safe for you.

Where to Buy Them

The first step in getting colored contacts is seeing an optician. An eye care professional can make sure that colored contacts are safe for you and write you a prescription. Follow the advice of an eye care professional before listening to anything you read online.

One site that we use to buy colored contacts is PinkyParadise. They require a prescription and have FDA-approved lenses. There are many other sites that cosplayers use to purchase contacts. Make sure to read reviews and buy from reputable brands. The safest place to buy colored contacts is directly from your optician.

How to Wear Contacts

Wear contacts for only a short amount of time. Never go to sleep, shower, or go swimming in them. Seriously—you can end up with life-altering eye damage. Keep a bottle of rewetting drops such as Refresh® Relieva™ handy and an empty lens case with you at all times while wearing lenses. If your eyes become painful or irritated, take out the contacts. Always double check the expiration date before putting in contacts.

Putting in Contacts

1. When you first open your contacts, you'll want to soak them in a contact solution for at least eight hours before putting them on.

2. Wash and dry your hands thoroughly.

3. Use the pad of your pointer finger to pick up the lens. Don't use your nails as that can damage the lens.

4. Inspect the lens for defects such as chipping, wrinkled edges, or tears. Don't use them if they're damaged in any way. Make sure there is no grime or hair on the lens. Clean them with contact disinfectant if there is.

5. Check the lens shape to make sure the contact isn't inside out. Look at it from the side. The lens should be shaped like a bowl. If it's inside out, the edges will flare out.

6. When putting in the lens, I find it helpful to hold open my upper eyelid using the middle finger of my non-dominant hand.

7. Then I use the middle finger on my dominant hand, with the contact on my pointer finger, to hold down my lower lid.

8. Gently tap the lens directly on the cornea.

9. Don't get discouraged if it takes several tries. Some people find putting a single drop of solution onto the lens makes it more comfortable.

10. Once the lens is fully on the eye, blink a few times to center the contact on the iris.

Contact Lens Upkeep

Appropriately clean and store your contact lenses. Never clean or store them with regular water. Some of the worst contact-related eye infections are related to using regular water with contacts. Use disinfectant solution specifically made for contacts. Our favorite is Biotrue® Multi-Purpose contact lens solution.

Pay attention to when the contact lenses expire. Writing the expiration date on your lens case can be a good way to keep track of it. Make sure to regularly change the contact solution in your lens case. If your contact lens case leaks and your contact lenses dry out, throw away the contacts. Attempting to rehydrate and reuse them will put your eyes at risk.

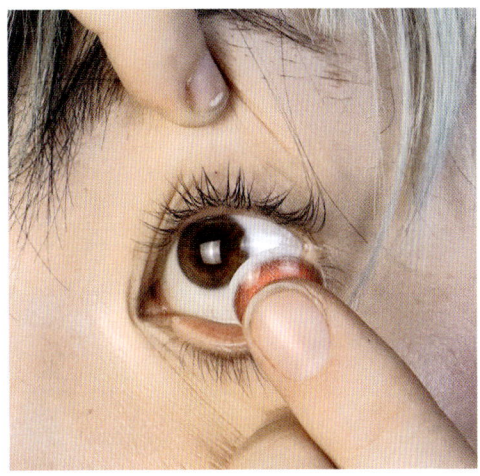

Holding the Eye and Putting in the Lens

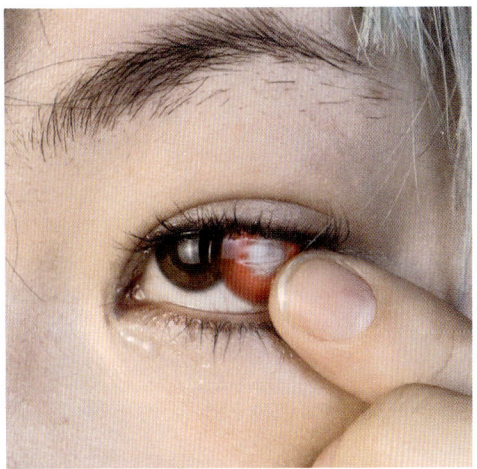

Misplaced Lens on the Cornea

FABRIC AND FRILLS

Now we get to the "cos" part of cosplay: the costumes! You can buy, alter, create, and commission. There are endless ways of sourcing the right garments for your desired look.

BUYING COSTUMES

Making costumes from scratch has its pros and cons. Thrifting and altering can be affordable, but sometimes it's challenging to create a canonically accurate cosplay of a character. However, buying the materials, tools, and craft space to make costumes entirely from scratch can be daunting and expensive. While we love sewing our own costumes, it sometimes makes more economic sense to buy them outright or buy clothes to alter.

BUYING COSPLAYS ONLINE

If you're cosplaying a character who has a very popular design, you might be able to order a mass-manufactured version of the costume online. There are plenty of websites to choose from that all vary in price and quality.

Wish, AliExpress, and Temu® might have the best prices, but shipping time can sometimes take months and the quality might be questionable. We recommend you do a thorough research on reviews before purchasing from any of these companies. Oftentimes with shipping prices, it might be more worthwhile to order from a different company.

For the most affordable mass-manufactured cosplays with the best quality and return policies, I usually prefer Miccostumes. Other companies like DokiDoki Cosplay and EZcosplay also have a large selection and affordable prices. When purchasing from these websites, always read the reviews on the specific cosplay you're purchasing to make sure the sizing and photos are accurate.

Tip: A lot of mass-manufactured cosplay companies are not size inclusive. Always read the measurements of a garment before purchasing.

You can also purchase cosplays secondhand online. EBay and Mercari are great options for secondhand cosplays!

BUYING COSPLAYS IN PERSON

Finding cosplays in person can be challenging, but not impossible. As the cosplay hobby has grown in popularity, some mainstream companies carry cosplay costumes around Halloween. Spirit Halloween and Walmart both have small sections dedicated to anime or comic books. You might also be fortunate enough to have a year-round costume store in your area that carries pre-made cosplays or costume pieces.

In-person stores will carry a very limited quantity of cosplays, and their quality might be subpar. However, the benefit is that you are able to see the costume in person before buying it, and in some cases try the pieces on.

ORDERING COMMISSIONS

Commissions are cosplays made by small designers to your exact measurements. Commissions can be very expensive, but if you are unable to make your own cosplays and want a polished product, they're a great option! There are numerous amazing commissioners out there, but do your research to make sure they are reputable!

CUSTOMIZING FABRIC COLOR

Sometimes you might find the perfect article of clothing, but it's the wrong color. Dyeing fabric might feel intimidating, but it's actually very straightforward. There are three commonly used types of fabric dye. The type of dye you use depends on the fabric you are working with. Always read the fabric composition on the tag before dyeing anything.

All-purpose dye: All-purpose dye is typically used with natural fiber fabrics such as 100% cotton, wool, linen, or silk.

Synthetic dye: Synthetic dye is used for fabric with synthetic fibers, such as polyester and acetate. Cotton/polyester blends should be dyed with synthetic dye.

Leather dye: Leather dye is an amazing way to recolor real leather. Keep in mind that leather dye will *not* work on pleather or vegan leather.

Color remover: Color remover is meant to be used on colored fabric prior to dyeing. It is meant for fabrics such as cotton, linen, silk, wool, ramie and rayon. It is not meant to be used on polyester.

TUTORIAL

STOVETOP DYEING

Most fabric can be dyed with the correct technique, but it can be intimidating to try and dye something yourself. Before dyeing your fabric, keep a few things in mind. First, you cannot lighten fabric with fabric dye. You need to choose a color darker than the fabric you are starting with. Second, the undertones of the fabric will affect the final color. For example, if you are dyeing a light blue shirt red, the result might be purple. Use color theory when dyeing fabric. If you are new to dyeing fabric, it's best to stick to dyeing white fabric to avoid botched end results.

WHAT YOU NEED

Fabric to be dyed

Stovetop

A large pot

Fabric dye of choice

Salt or white vinegar (if instructed by product label)

1. Wet your fabric. This will make it easier to get an even dye job. If you dip dry fabric into boiling dye, the end result could end up patchy and uneven.

2. Mix your water in a large pot following the instructions and measurements on the fabric dye. For some types of fabric, the instructions might recommend mixing the fabric dye with either salt or vinegar.

3. Bring your dye mixture to a boil. Carefully place your fabric into the water and stir, making sure the fabric is fully saturated. Stir continuously for up to one hour or until the desired color is achieved. Note that the fabric will appear darker when wet.

4. Rinse under cold water in the sink to lock the color in.

Tip: Instead of carrying the entire pot to the sink, use an empty bucket or bowl to move the fabric to avoid making a mess.

5. Either in the sink or in the washing machine, wash the garment with cold water and laundry detergent to prevent any dye from bleeding out of the fabric. Allow the piece to dry completely. And you're done!

TUTORIAL
OMBRÉ DYEING

Ombré dyeing should be done on the stovetop. This is similar to stovetop dyeing (page 101), but instead of dyeing an entire fabric the same color, you'll make a gradient. Continue until you achieve the desired color.

WHAT YOU NEED

Fabric to be dyed

Stovetop

A large pot

Fabric dye of choice

Salt or white vinegar (if instructed by product label)

1. Wet your fabric. This will make it easier to get an even dye job. If you dip dry fabric into boiling dye, the end result could end up patchy and uneven.

2. Mix your water in a large pot following the instructions and measurements on the fabric dye. For some types of fabric, the instructions might recommend mixing the fabric dye with either salt or vinegar.

3. Bring your dye mixture to a boil. Carefully hold your fabric above the dye mixture, then dip the end of the fabric you want the darkest into the dye. Move the fabric in and out of the mixture continuously. Be careful not to hold the fabric still, as this will compromise the gradient. Note that the fabric will appear darker when wet.

4. Rinse under cold water in the sink to lock the color in.

Tip: Instead of carrying the entire pot to the sink, use an empty bucket or bowl to move the fabric to avoid making a mess.

5. Either in the sink or in the washing machine, wash the garment with cold water and laundry detergent to prevent any dye from bleeding out of the fabric. Allow the piece to dry completely. And you're done!

TUTORIAL

DYEING A FULL GARMENT IN THE WASHING MACHINE

If you don't have a large pot, it can be tricky to dye a full garment on the stovetop. Dyeing garments using the washing machine is super easy because the machine does most of the work! Fabric dye will *not* ruin your washing machine. Keep in mind that dyeing using the washing machine will not work on synthetic fabrics such as polyester blends.

WHAT YOU WILL NEED

Garment of choice

Washing machine

Dish detergent

All-purpose fabric dye

2 large bowls or buckets

Salt, if dyeing cotton, linen, ramie, or rayon

Vinegar, if dyeing nylon, silk, or wool

Bleach

Old towels or scrap fabric

1. Wet your fabric in the sink and place it in the washing machine.

2. Set your washing machine to hot and set the cycle time to at least 45 minutes.

3. Add one teaspoon of dish detergent and start the cycle.

4. Measure your fabric dye according to the instructions on the package. Mix with 4 cups (960 ml) of water in a large bowl.

5. In another large bowl, mix 4 cups (960 ml) of hot water with 1 cup (288 g) of salt or 1 cup (240 ml) of vinegar, depending on the type of fabric.

6. Pour both mixtures into the detergent dispenser. Flush clean with 4 cups (960 ml) of hot water. Finish the cycle.

7. Rewash the item with laundry detergent in warm water.

8. Dry your garment and it is ready to wear! I always prefer to air-dry my garments to avoid shrinking.

9. Clean your washing machine by wiping around the lid. Run the machine for a full cycle on hot with 2 cups (480 ml) of bleach and a few dirty rags.

TUTORIAL

DYEING REAL LEATHER

Dyeing natural leather is very simple, and can be especially helpful for customizing secondhand leather pieces. For my Mario cosplay, I dyed a secondhand brown leather vest. Leather dye is a special type of dye with an application sponge at the end. Leather dye will *not* work on synthetic pleather.

WHAT YOU WILL NEED

Leather

Cardboard (optional)

Leather dye

Protective gloves (optional)

1. Lay your leather down onto a flat surface.

Tip: An easy way to protect the surface you're working on is with spare cardboard!

2. Shake your bottle of leather dye and gently open it to pull out the applicator sponge.

3. Slowly press the sponge onto the leather to dye the desired section. The color will change immediately.

4. Allow the leather to dry to see the final color. For a deeper color, apply multiple layers. Allow each layer to dry before applying another. Once your leather is dry, you're done! You do not need to rinse out the leather dye.

ADDING SMALL DETAILS

Some cosplay designs have small details on the fabric. There are countless ways to create these details. Experienced cosplayers might use their Cricut® vinyl or embroidery, but for newer cosplayers without access to those machines there are a few simple ways to create these details with minimal experience.

Fabric Paint

Fabric paint is extremely affordable and has many different uses. While fabric paint is a similar consistency to acrylic paint, it's different in a few ways—the main difference being that you can wash it without the paint bleeding into the garment.

Fabric paint can be extremely unforgiving as it is nearly impossible to get out once it touches fabric, so be very careful while handling it near your garment. Fabric paint will also crack over time and make your costume very stiff. Never use fabric paint in lieu of fabric dye when covering an entire garment.

There are a few different types of fabric paint, each with their own uses.

Basic fabric paint: These typically come in small bottles and come in a large variety of colors, including metallics.

Fabric spray paint: Fabric spray paint is extremely helpful for covering large areas with consistent opaque color.

Puff paint: Puff paint, once dry, expands to have a puffy texture.

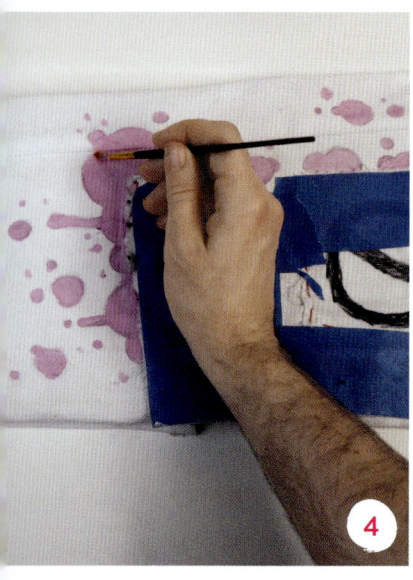

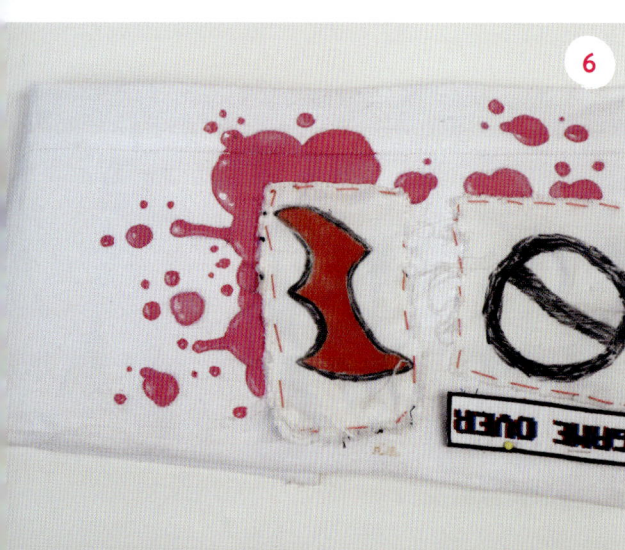

TUTORIAL

CREATING SMALL SYMBOLS WITH FABRIC PAINT

Fabric paint is helpful for adding small, original symbols onto your garment. It's also a good replacement if you do not have access to iron-on transfers or vinyl.

WHAT YOU WILL NEED

Cardboard

Garment

Pencil

Painter's tape

Fabric paint

Assorted brushes

Water

Paper towel

1. Place the cardboard on the inside of the garment to protect the other side. Fabric paint will bleed while wet. If you do not protect the inside of your garment, it will bleed to the other side.

2. Draw your design with a pencil.

3. Use painter's tape to protect the area around your design.

4. Start painting! I usually prefer to start with the primary color of the design. Once each full layer is complete, let it dry completely before applying another. It's a long process, but it will have great results. Clean and dry your brushes with paper towels in between each layer.

5. Switch colors and apply small details. If you make a mistake and your small detail is too large, don't worry! You can paint over fabric paint and redo any details.

6. Once the paint is completely dry, remove the tape and it's ready to wear!

TUTORIAL

ADDING OMBRÉ DETAILS WITH FABRIC PAINT

Not all ombré details can be made with fabric dye. Some small details need to be painted on. This is an organic process, so you will not be drawing on the design. Prepare your reference image prior to starting.

WHAT YOU WILL NEED

Garment

Cardboard

Assorted brushes

Fabric paint

Paper towel

Water

Fabric spray paint (optional)

1. Lay your garment down on the cardboard. Place more cardboard on the inside of the fabric to protect it from any bleeding paint.

2. Using a flat brush, pick up some of your fabric paint and dab it onto some scrap cardboard to create a dry brushing effect. Dab the brush onto the areas of the garment where you want the paint to be the darkest, working in small sections at a time.

3. Blend the paint into the garment in the desired direction. You can do this with another brush, a sponge, or even a paper towel!

4. Repeat steps 2 and 3 until the section is completely finished. You can layer other colors at this time to give a more dynamic look!

5. (Optional) For large areas of fabric, try fabric spray paint!

6. Allow to dry completely and the paint is complete!

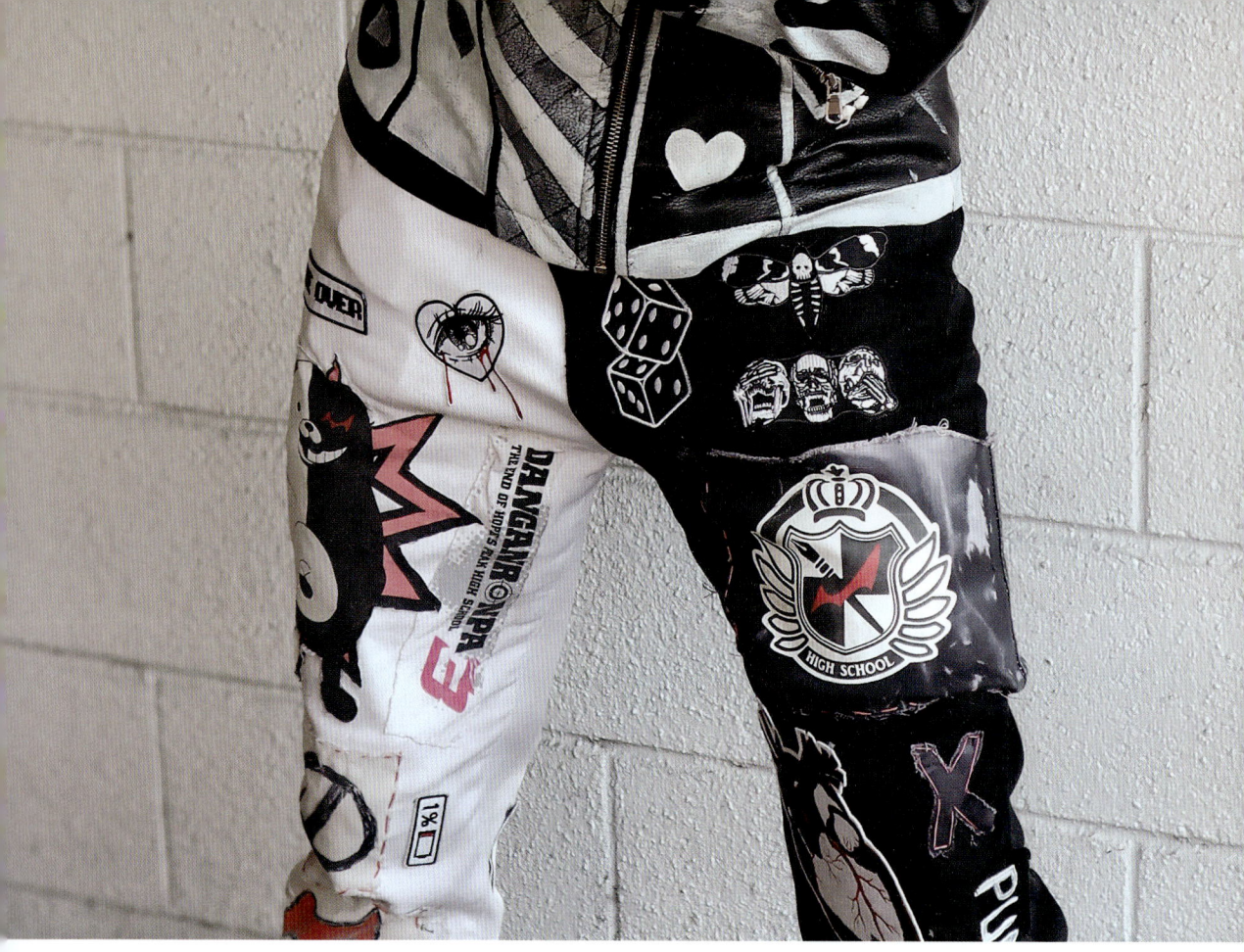

IRON-ONS

Some complicated details can be printed and ironed directly onto your fabric. These are called fabric transfers. There are two kinds of iron-on fabric transfers: light and dark. Light transfers are meant almost exclusively for white fabric. Dark transfers can be used on any color. For best results, use fabric transfers exclusively on cotton or cotton-blend fabrics. Note that if you are using *light* transfers, you need to mirror the image before printing the design.

TUTORIAL

FABRIC TRANSFERS

Some complicated details can be printed and ironed directly onto your fabric. These are called fabric transfers. There are two kinds of iron-on fabric transfers: light and dark. Light transfers are meant almost exclusively for white fabric. Dark transfers can be used on any color. For best results, use fabric transfers exclusively on cotton or cotton-blend fabrics. Note: If you are using light transfers, you need to mirror the image before printing the design.

WHAT YOU WILL NEED

Design

Iron-on transfer paper

Color printer

Scissors

Garment

Pillowcase or scrap fabric

Iron

Tip: If you can't find a sheet of paper, you can use a thin piece of cotton scrap fabric!

4a

1. Download and test the size of your design. Iron-on transfers can be expensive, so you want to print out your design in black and white to test the size before printing it onto your fabric transfer.

2. Once your design is printed in the right size, you can print it onto your fabric transfer. Check your printer settings to make sure you are printing the design onto the blank side of the transfer sheet.

3. Cut out your transfer, ensuring the design is cut perfectly. If there are any white sections missed, this could affect the end result.

4. Lay your garment down perfectly flat on a countertop or other completely flat surface. *Do not use an ironing board.* Protect your surface with a pillowcase or scrap fabric.

For light transfers: Place the design face down onto your garment. Set your iron to high and turn off any steam. Iron on the transfer for 2–3 minutes, making sure you use heavy pressure. Once the design is completely cool, peel off the back sticker and you're done!

For dark transfers: Carefully peel the back of the transfer off and place the design onto your garment. Dark fabric transfers usually come with a protective sheet of paper. Place this on top of your design. Iron on the transfer for 2–3 minutes, making sure you use heavy pressure. Once the design is cool, it is ready to wear!

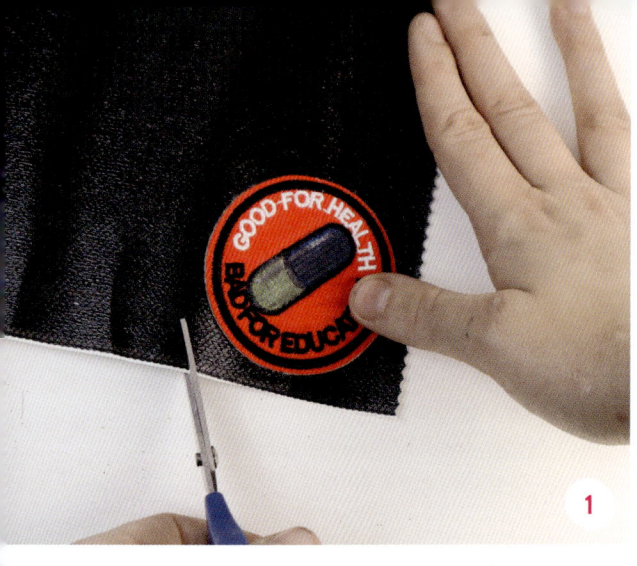

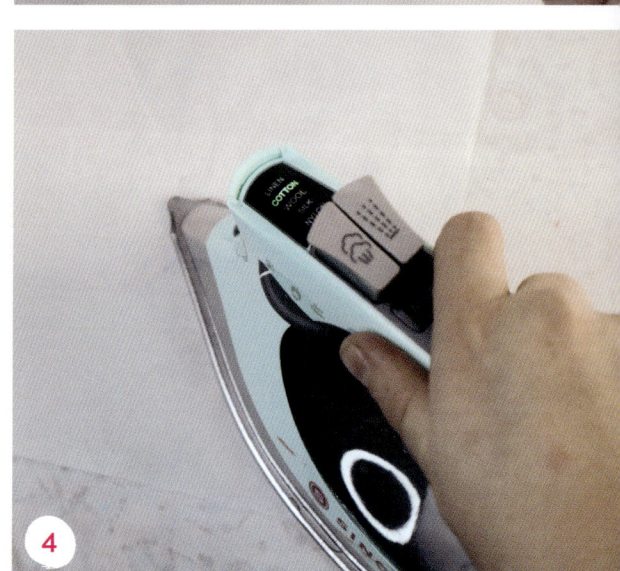

TUTORIAL

PATCHES

If a character is popular enough or the design is simple enough, you might be able to find iron-on patches of whatever details you need. There are two types of patches you can buy: iron-on and sew-on. Iron-on patches are more beginner-friendly, but there is actually a technique you can use to turn any patch into an iron-on patch. If you do manage to find an iron-on patch for your cosplay, see step 6.

WHAT YOU WILL NEED

Patch
HeatnBond® UltraHold
Pencil
Scissors
Pillowcase or scrap fabric
Iron
Garment

1. Lay your patch down on your HeatnBond. Using a pencil, trace the shape of your patch onto the material.

2. Cut the HeatnBond following your outline.

3. Place the patch face down onto a hard surface, using a pillowcase or other thin fabric to protect the surface. For best results, do not use an ironing board. Place the cut HeatnBond bumpy side–down onto the patch.

4. Using your iron on medium heat, firmly press the HeatnBond onto the patch and hold for ten seconds.

5. Once the patch is cool, remove the sticker backing on the back of the HeatnBond.

6. Place your patch face up on your garment, ensuring it's in the right position. Using medium heat, firmly press your iron onto the patch and hold for ten seconds.

7. Allow to cool completely. Test to see if the patch is completely secured. If it isn't, repeat step 6.

TUTORIAL

IRON-ON VINYL

A lot of experienced cosplayers use Cricut machines, but did you know you can use Cricut's iron-on materials without a Cricut? For simple designs, it's possible to purchase iron-on vinyl intended for these cutting machines and draw your own designs.

WHAT YOU WILL NEED

Stencil

Pencil

Iron-on vinyl

Scissors or X-ACTO® knife

Scrap fabric

Iron

Tweezers

Fabric

1. Using a stencil, draw your design onto the shiny side of the vinyl. *Make sure your design is mirrored.*

2. Cut out the design.

3. Place the design plastic side up onto the garment and lay on a heat-resistant flat surface. *Do not use an ironing board; it is better to use a countertop.*

4. Place your scrap fabric over the design to protect it and iron the design on medium-high heat, being careful not to burn your fabric. Do not use steam.

5. After the design has completely cooled, use your tweezers to check every corner of the design to make sure it has successfully transferred to the fabric. If one corner isn't sticking, repeat step 4 until the design is secure.

6. Fully remove the plastic layer and your design is complete!

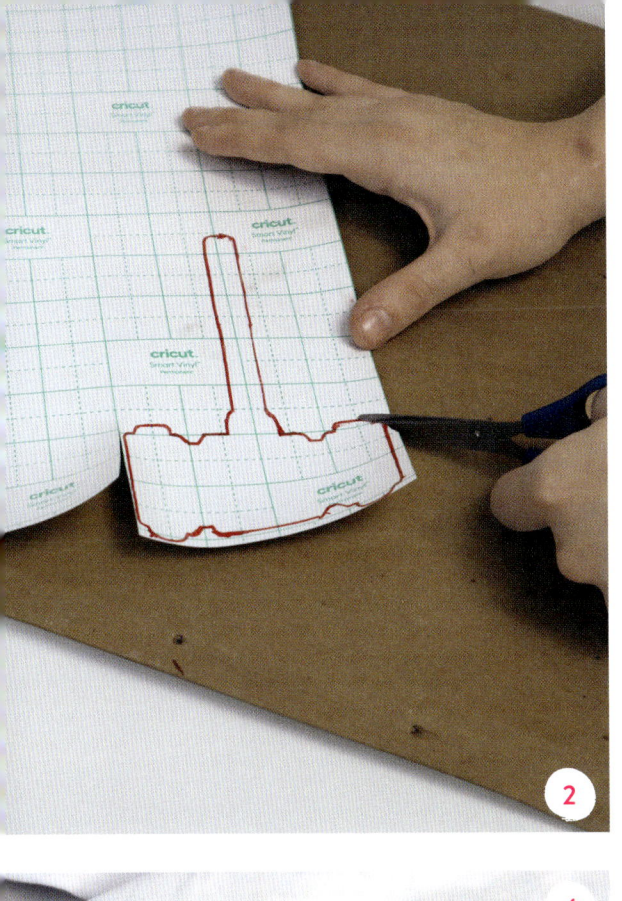

WEATHERING

Weathering is when you intentionally age or distress a costume to make it appear worn. It might seem strange to intentionally damage your costume. However, when you imagine a war-torn hero, do you picture a pristine outfit? Likely not! They would have grime from battles. A worn look can make a character more believable.

Weathering can help your costume look more realistic and unique. It is especially useful for store-bought costumes. It can give the impression of high-quality materials or intricate details without the cost of a handmade costume. Distressed costumes often look more visually interesting and dynamic, helping the character stand out. The goal is to create a more realistic look that reflects the character's background or experiences.

There are many methods for weathering your costume. Feel free to get creative and try new ways. Here are some of our favorite options.

STAINING FABRIC

Tea or coffee staining: This works best on lighter colored fabrics. Soak the fabric in a mixture of brewed tea or coffee to give it a yellowed, aged look. Rinse and dry. Repeat the process as needed.

Grime: Face makeup, charcoal, or even real dirt can be used to create stains and smudges. Rub the dirt into the fabric. Apply gradually in layers for a more realistic effect.

CREATING FRAYS AND TEARS

Sandpaper: Lightly rub areas of the fabric to create a frayed or worn effect. Fabric tends to naturally wear down in areas with more friction such as knees, elbows, hems, edges, and seams. Be careful not to go too far with this; you don't want your garment to look like Swiss cheese.

Burning: Be extremely careful if you want to attempt adding burns. Only attempt on organic materials, not synthetics. Synthetic fibers like polyester, acetate, and nylon can melt under high heat and produce hazardous fumes.

Strategic cuts: Carefully make small cuts or tears in the fabric. Focus on high-friction areas like elbows and knees.

TUTORIAL

WEATHERING FAKE LEATHER

Fake leather is made from plastic, and it doesn't wear down over time in the same way that real leather does. It cannot be dyed or stained, so we will need to use a painting technique.

WHAT YOU WILL NEED

Fake leather item, such as a costume, prop, or accessory

Rubbing alcohol, for cleaning

Sandpaper, fine or medium grit

Sponge or brush

Acrylic-based paint

Cloth for wiping excess paint

Clear matte acrylic sealer, brush-on or spray (optional)

1. Clean the fake leather by wiping the item with rubbing alcohol. This will help the paint adhere better.

2. Use sandpaper to gently sand areas where wear would occur such as edges, seams, and high-friction spots.

3. For base color application, use a sponge to apply a thin layer of a color slightly darker than your item's original color. It's okay if the paint is uneven; the goal is to create a varied texture.

4. Use a sponge to apply a thin layer of a color matching the item's original shade. This layering will add extra dimension.

5. Pick a much lighter shade for highlights. To dry brush the highlights, dip a stiff brush or dry sponge in the lighter paint. Remove most of the paint by wiping with a cloth. Lightly brush over raised areas and edges to create highlights.

6. Add depth with darker shades. The darker you go, the more dramatic and even cartoony the final look will be. Use the dry brush technique to apply the dark paint to creases, seams, and areas that would gather dirt or wear.

7. (Optional) Once everything is dry, apply clear acrylic sealer. Both brush-on and spray works. Apply in a well-ventilated area.

See final picture on page 118.

2

3

4

5

6a

6b 6c

ADDING SPIKES

• •

You may find the perfect jacket for a look that is missing that alternative edge to it. Worry not! It's super easy to add metal spikes to clothing and accessories if you have the proper supplies. Screw-back spikes can be found cheaply online and at many craft stores.

FABRIC AND FRILLS

123

TUTORIAL

CUSTOMIZING LEATHER WITH SPIKES

What better way to add some edge to your character than to add a few spikes to the outfit! This method for adding spikes is super easy. Add them to a leather jacket, vest, belt, handbag, etc. So long as you have the right tools, the creative options are endless.

WHAT YOU WILL NEED

Marker

Garment

Awl or X-ACTO knife

Screw-back studs or spikes

1. Using a marker, make note of where you want the spikes coming out of your garment.

2. Use your awl to pierce the fabric where the spike will go. If you don't have an awl, an X-ACTO knife can also work. Just be careful not to make the hole too large or your spike won't stay in place. The hole should be just large enough to fit the screw bottom of the spikes.

3. Push the screw bottom of the spike through the hole from underneath the garment.

4. Once the screw is fully in place, screw the top half of the spike onto the bottom piece. This will sandwich the garment in between the two pieces of metal.

5. The screw is fully attached! Repeat the process for as many spikes as you need.

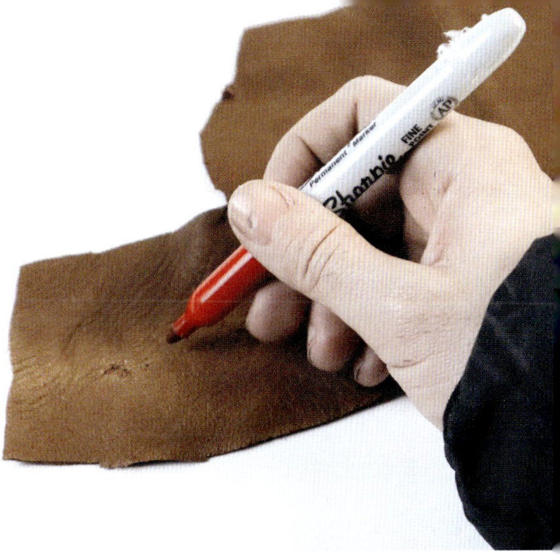

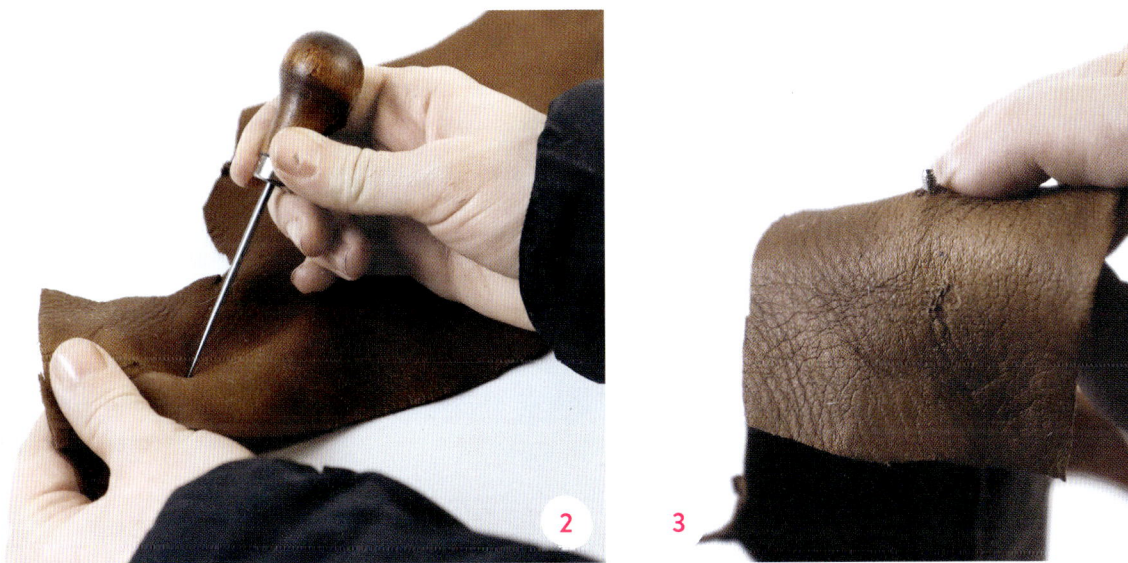
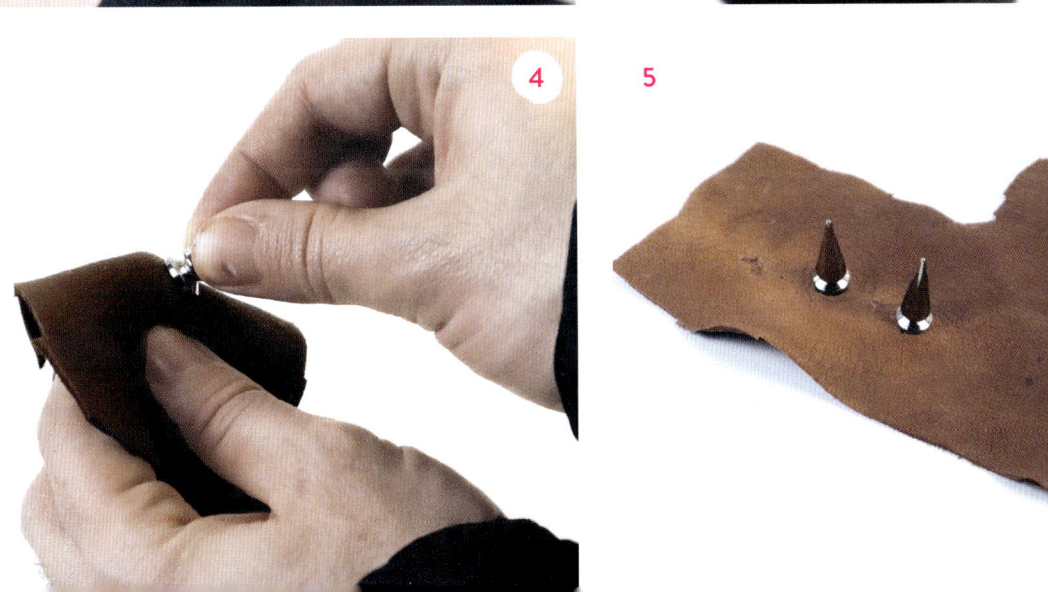

CUSTOMIZING FOOTWEAR

Cosplay shoes are extremely expensive and can often be horrible for your feet. If you're wearing a costume to a convention, it's important to have a complete, but comfortable look. I prefer to customize my own footwear.

TUTORIAL

GEMS, BOWS, AND MORE

What better way to make shoes cute than to add a big bow? The method for gluing bows can be used for many large details, such as gems, flowers, and more!

WHAT YOU WILL NEED

Shoes

Disposable gloves (optional)

E6000 PLUS glue

Cotton swab

Accessory to be attached, such as a bow

Strong clips

1. Wipe down the area of the shoe where you plan on attaching the accessory. A clean surface will help the item stay attached longer.

2. If desired, put on disposable gloves to protect your hands. Apply a small amount of E6000 PLUS glue directly onto the shoe. Spread evenly with the cotton swab and allow it to dry for ten seconds.

3. Firmly press the accessory onto the desired spot. Use strong clips to hold the item in place. Allow to set for at least 24 hours.

4. Once the glue is completely set, the shoe is ready to be worn!

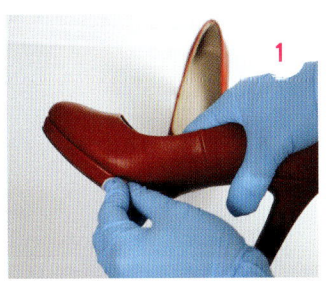

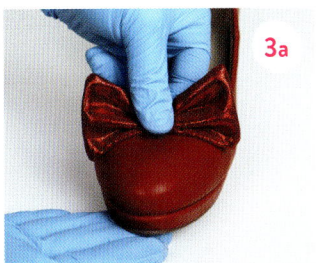

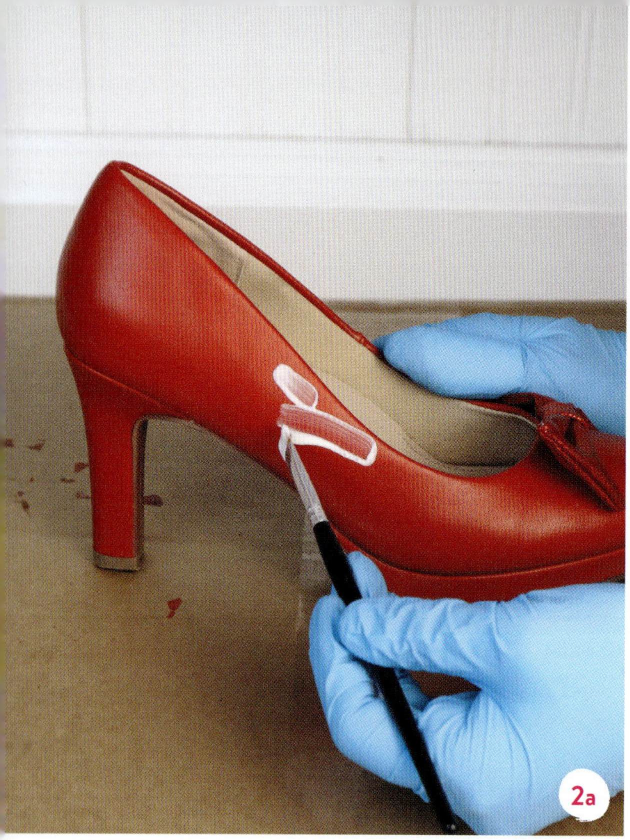

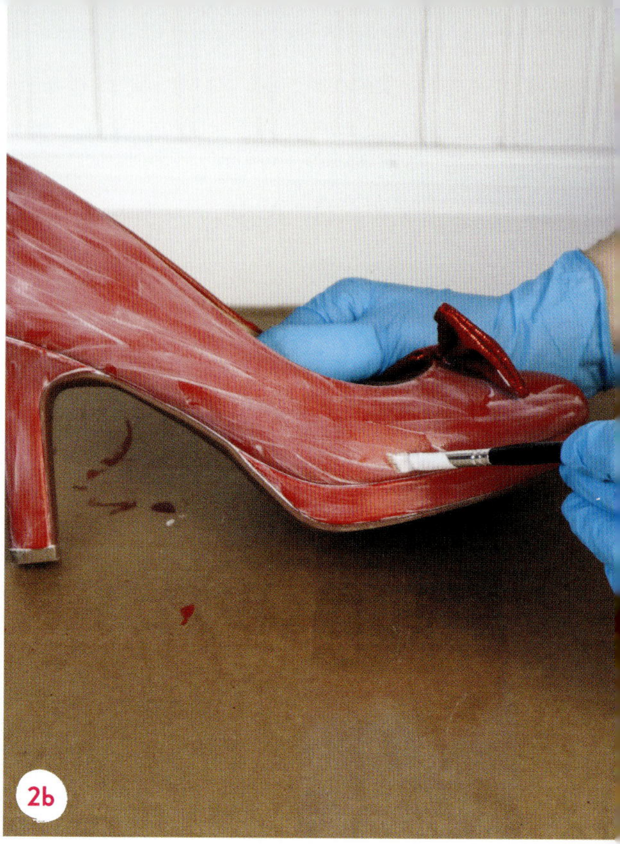

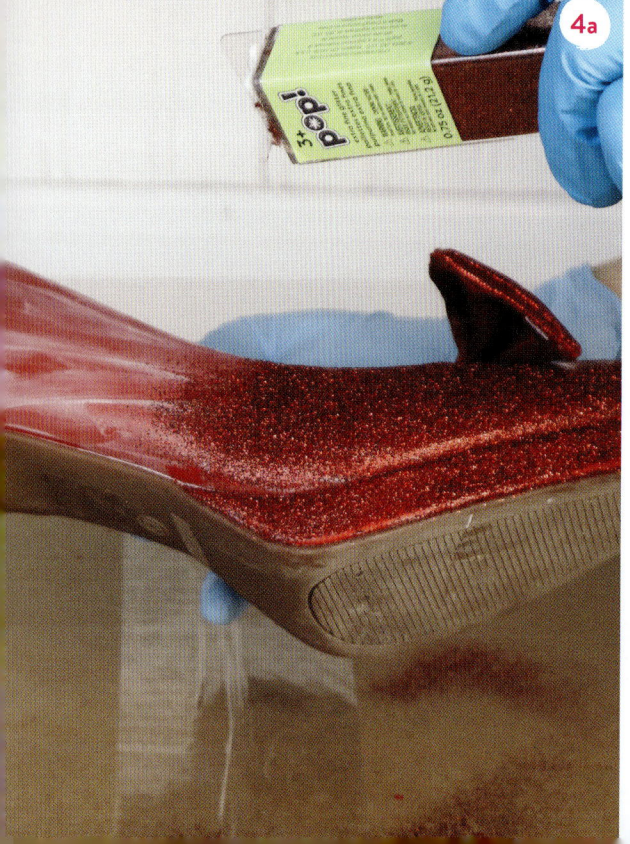

TUTORIAL

GLITTER

Sometimes you can find shoes that are almost perfect, but are missing the pizzazz needed for the final look. For these looks, it might be time to add glitter!

Adding glitter onto shoes is done using glue. For best results, use leather or faux leather shoes for gluing on glitter. Stretchy material could result in a patchy finish.

WHAT YOU WILL NEED

Shoes

Washcloth

Disposable paint brush

Mod Podge® Matte

Paper plates or cardboard

Glitter

Spray-on enamel

1. Clean your shoes. Even if they are new, gently cleaning them with a washcloth will remove any dirt and grime, resulting in a cleaner finish.

2. Paint the Mod Podge all over the shoes in a thin, even layer. Avoid clumps or thick patches of glue.

3. Place the gluey shoes onto paper plates, cardboard, or another disposable vessel.

4. Sprinkle glitter onto the shoes. Make sure to catch any fallen glitter. Dump the excess glitter captured on the paper plates into a new vessel and repeat until the desired opaqueness is achieved.

5. Dry the shoes overnight. Then, stomp the shoes onto the ground to shake off any excess glitter. After that, spray the shoes with a thin layer of gloss enamel to protect the layer of glitter. Allow to dry and the shoes are ready to wear!

See final image on page 126.

TUTORIAL

ADDING RIBBON

Ballerina-type shoes often have ribbons crisscrossing from the base of the foot to the top of the calf. This kind of alteration can be done easily without damaging the external part of the shoe!

WHAT YOU WILL NEED

Shoes

Washcloth

Ribbon

Pencil

Cotton swab

Shoe Goo® or E6000 PLUS glue

Disposable gloves

Strong clips

1. Clean the inside of the shoe to the best of your ability using a damp washcloth. Dry completely before continuing.

2. Measure the length of ribbon you need for each leg. If you are crisscrossing the ribbon around your leg, measure the ribbon on your leg before cutting to avoid cutting it too short. Cut two even sections of ribbon according to these measurements.

3. Put on your shoes. Using a pencil, mark where you want the ribbons to start. They will most commonly start just beneath the ankle bone.

4. Using a cotton swab, spread a smooth, thin layer of Shoe Goo onto the inside of the shoe from the pencil mark to the base of the sole. Allow to dry for ten seconds until it is tacky.

5. Wearing gloves, firmly press the ribbon onto the glued surface. Make sure to smooth the ribbon, especially at the base of the shoe.

6. Use strong clips to hold the ribbon in place and allow to dry for at least 24 hours. Once the glue is dry, the ribbon is ready to be tied and worn.

4

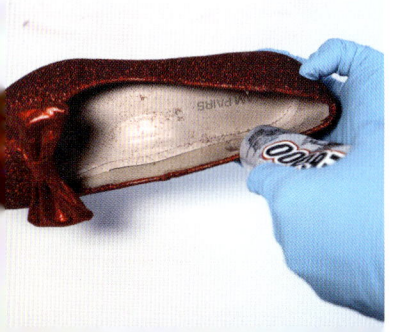

5

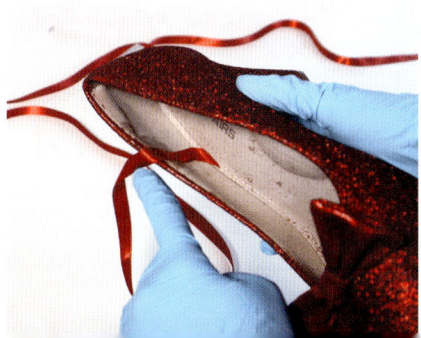

6

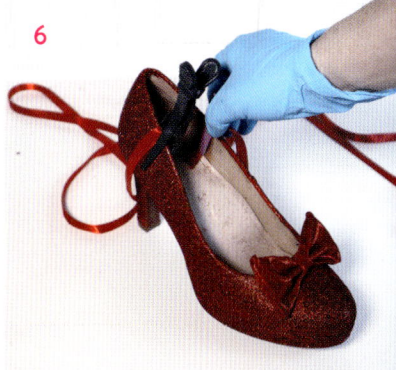

1a

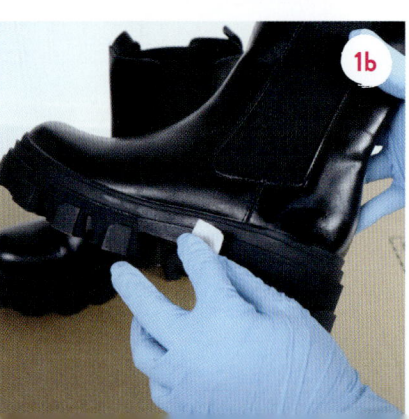
1b

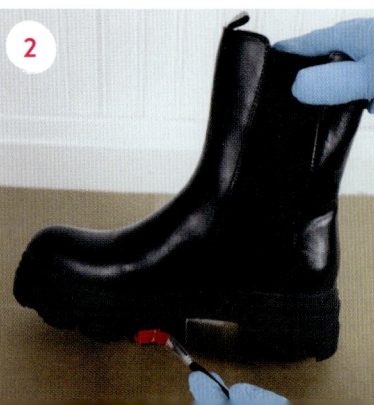
2

TUTORIAL

PAINTING FOOTWEAR

When a character has small colorful details on their shoes, it's simple to paint these directly onto the shoes. Not just any paint will work on shoes. If you use plain acrylic paint, the paint will crack and chip as you walk around. The most popular brand for painting shoes is Angelus Direct®.

WHAT YOU WILL NEED

Shoes

Rag or paper towel

Acetone

Brushes

Angelus Direct acrylic leather paint

Angelus Direct acrylic finisher, satin finish or spray gloss enamel

1. Using a rag or paper towel, clean the shoes with acetone to prep the surface for the paint.

2. Begin painting one layer at a time. Allow each layer to dry completely before beginning the next.

3. Once the last layer is completely dry, use a small brush to touch up any flawed details. Using a finishing coat or enamel spray, coat the paint to give it a polished shine.

4. Once the shoe is dry it's ready to wear!

THE ♥♥ KITCHEN SINK! (EVERYTHING ELSE)

The rest of your cosplay might have props, crowns, horns, and other miscellaneous pieces! This is where you can get creative! Knowing how to make props and accessories can be a huge skill, but there are some basics involving foam work and paint that could make the process a lot easier.

BASIC FOAM WORK

Foam work can seem intimidating if you've never done it before. Many amazing cosplayers make their props out of something called EVA foam. EVA foam is a high-density craft foam with very few air bubbles. With the right supplies and techniques, working with EVA foam is actually very straightforward. Here is a breakdown of different supplies you might use while making or altering props.

EVA foam: EVA foam is a high-density craft foam with a variety of uses. It comes in various sizes and thickness. EVA foam can be purchased from a variety of in-person craft stores. Coscom Cosplay Supplies is a good online option for affordability and quality.

X-ACTO knife: X-ACTO knives are extremely helpful for cutting a variety of craft materials without leaving marks. It's important to switch out the blade regularly. Cutting anything with a dull blade increases the likelihood of injury.

Contact cement: Contact cement is the best glue to use on EVA foam. The best brands of this are Barge All Purpose Cement and Weldwood® Original Contact Cement. Never use the low-odor or any specialty formulas.

Heat gun: Any standard heat gun will do. Heat guns are much hotter than hair dryers and are not interchangeable. Be very careful while handling. Always use a heat gun on top of a burn-resistant surface.

Dremel: You can find a dremel at any hardware store or online. They usually come with a wide variety of bits that are interchangeable for different projects. For foam work, you will use the sanding bits the most.

Precision heat tool: Most projects will not need heat pens. We use these for adding fine details to foam projects. Always handle heat tools with care to avoid injury.

Kwik Seal®: Kwik Seal is actually used in plumbing as a type of caulk! It's extremely useful for filling and covering small visible seams or gaps in the foam you glue together. You can find this at most hardware stores.

Sandpaper: Sheets of fine sandpaper help smooth out a prop.

Disposable brushes: Some small containers of contact cement have an application brush attached to the lid. If you're using a large can of cement, it's best to stock up on disposable brushes. You can use acid brushes sold at hardware stores, or even cheap children's paint brushes.

Respirator: You will need to wear a respirator any time you use a dremel or heat tool, apply contact cement, or use spray paint. *Always* wear a respirator and work in a well-ventilated space. You can find protective respirators online or at hardware stores. Replace the filters when necessary.

Plasti Dip®: Plasti Dip is the best primer to use on EVA foam. It sprays on, so there are no brush streaks. It's also very durable. You can buy Plasti Dip in white or black.

Spray paint: I usually prefer doing a base of spray paint on my foam props to get the base to an even color, especially for metallic shades.

Acrylic paint: Acrylic paint is fast drying and perfect for props.

Worbla: Worbla is a thermoplastic sheet that can be molded using a heat gun. It's expensive, but very durable. You can buy Worbla or similar brands online, as it can be challenging to find brick and mortar sellers.

Enamel topcoat: I prefer most of my props to have a glossy finish. Clear enamel is the best topcoat. It won't show streaks, and it's great at protecting the paint.

Mod Podge: Mod Podge also works as a topcoat. Mod Podge might show brush streaks, but it's very affordable.

Hot glue gun: Hot glue can be used for a variety of things. The glue itself is not very strong, but it can be used to glue on a variety of non-structural details, fabric, and clips. Any standard hot glue gun will do.

Small hair clips: You can buy these in bulk on Amazon. They're extremely useful for making and wearing accessories.

PATTERNING FOAM PROPS

You can find an affordable pattern for almost anything on sites like Etsy! I often buy patterns instead of trying to make them myself. However, for simple projects like spikes and crowns, it's pretty easy to draw the pattern out on paper and test the fit. Being able to visualize props and draw them as two-dimensional paper patterns does require a strong understanding of geometry. If you purchase a foam pattern, be sure to read the instructions and watch any accompanying videos before cutting out your foam.

TUTORIAL

MAKING A CROWN

Crowns come in a variety of shapes and sizes. For basic cartoon-style crowns, I always make them out of foam!

WHAT YOU WILL NEED

Foam pattern

Scissors

EVA foam, 2 mm

Marker

X-ACTO knife

Dremel with sanding bit

Heat gun

Respirator

Contact cement

Brush

Heat pen (optional)

Gemstones and painter's tape (optional)

Plasti Dip

Spray paint or acrylic paint

Glossy spray enamel

Clips

1. Prepare your foam pattern. I patterned this crown myself. Cut out the paper pattern and lay it down onto the EVA foam near the edge. Use a marker to trace the pattern onto the foam.

2. Cut out the pattern at a 90-degree angle, perpendicular to the floor using an X-ACTO knife.

(continued)

MAKING A CROWN (CONTINUED)

3. Check your work. If there are any large imperfections, use a sanding dremel. Gently drag the tool over the desired parts of the foam, carefully smoothing to remove any large uneven sections. If the EVA foam has been cut smoothly, skip this step.

4. Use your heat gun on high to shape the crown into a round shape, being careful not to burn yourself. Hold the foam in this shape as it cools.

5. Put on a respirator mask in a well-ventilated area. Glue the foam using contact cement. The trick to contact cement is patience. Using your brush, paint a thin layer of contact cement onto both ends of the foam crown. Wait for the contact cement to dry almost entirely. When the pieces are ready to be attached, the cement will be tacky to the touch. Do not try to attach the pieces when wet.

6. Using two hands, work your way from one end to another, firmly pressing together the glued edges. If done properly, the glue will immediately have a strong hold. You should not have to hold the foam pieces together while the crown dries. For best results, let the prop sit overnight for the glue to fully set.

7. (Optional) Add details. For this crown, I used my heat pen to draw some swirling texture details along various points of the crown. I also used contact cement to attach a few gems. If you attach gems, make sure to protect them using painter's tape before moving onto the next step.

8. Prime your foam using Plasti Dip. Make sure to shake your can thoroughly and apply a thin even layer. I usually spray one side at a time. Plasti Dip needs a few hours to cure in between layers, so this will be a long process. For best results, use at least 4–6 full layers.

9. Paint your prop! We have two different methods for painting crowns: spray paint and acrylic. Spray paint is much easier for those who are new to painting. Acrylic paint is more challenging, but it's less expensive and easier to achieve small details.

10. Seal the deal! Using a glossy spray enamel, spray a thin even layer all over the crown. This will give your prop a beautiful glossy shine, as well as protect your paint job from any damage.

11. Glue on some clips to the base of the crown. For small crowns, only two clips are necessary. I prefer having the clips facing opposite directions. This way you can twist the crown onto your hair, keeping it secure.

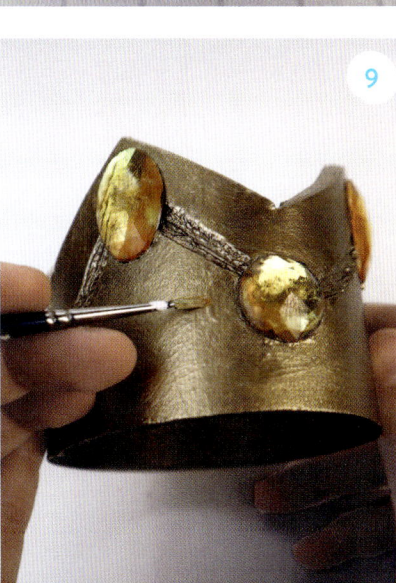

MAKING A FOAM SPIKE

Learning how to make an EVA foam cone spike is a great introduction to EVA foam crafting. These spikes can be added onto armor, garments, or even used as horns. You can use the skills you learn in this tutorial to move on to crafting more complicated foam props, armor, horns, and more. If you search online, you can purchase templates that will help you craft almost anything you can imagine.

For this tutorial, you will have two options. You can use the cone template we provide or you can follow our tutorial to learn how to make your own template. Learning to create your own cone template will give you freedom to make a variety of cone spike shapes.

There are a few different ways to attach foam spikes to a costume. A more advanced technique would be to sew magnets into the costume and glue magnets onto the spike. This way the spikes can be easily removed for easier washing. A more beginner-friendly option is to simply hot glue the spike onto the fabric. Be careful to avoid any glue showing!

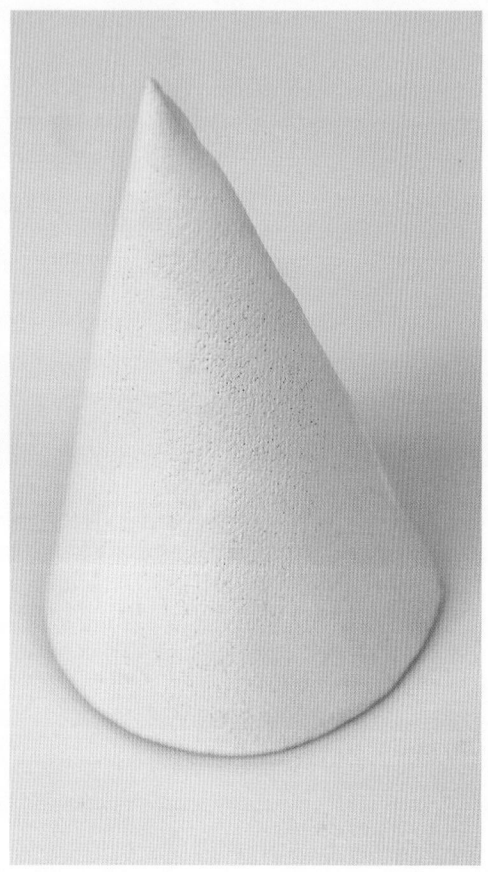

TUTORIAL

MAKING YOUR OWN SPIKE TEMPLATE

When it comes to crafting props and armor from foam, there's no shortage of templates and guides available online. Many cosplayers offer high-quality patterns at affordable prices, and we strongly encourage you to take advantage of these resources. Even with templates readily available, understanding how to create your own patterns is a useful skill. It's especially helpful when you want to customize a design to suit your needs. In this tutorial, we'll walk you through the process of creating a template for a foam spike, giving you the tools to shape and size it exactly how you envision.

WHAT YOU WILL NEED

Paper

Geometry compass to help you draw a circle, or a printout of a circle

Pencil

Ruler

Scissors

1. You will need a circle drawn on paper. You can print a circle out, trace around a circular object, or use a geometry compass to draw a circle. Keep in mind that the size of the circle will impact the size of your spike.

2. Mark the center of your circle. There are multiple ways to do this. I find the simplest method is to use a ruler to draw a square tightly framing the circle. Then draw an X from the corners. The intersection of the X is your center.

3. Cut out your circle.

4. Cut out a pizza-sized slice from your circle, with the point connecting to the center of the circle. The remaining part of the circle should look like Pac-Man.

5. Roll your paper template into a cone shape. You will be able to visualize the shape your foam spike will take. If the paper has to overlap to create the desired shape, that's a sign that you need to cut more pizza slices from your template.

6. If needed, cut more pizza slices from your template. Make sure to connect to the center point. Discard all the pizza slices.

7. With a pencil, write 45 degrees on the seam where the cone connects. Now you have your template!

See images and a traceable template example on pages 144 and 145.

MAKING YOUR OWN SPIKE TEMPLATE (CONTINUED)

TRACEABLE TEMPLATE EXAMPLE

TUTORIAL

HOW TO MAKE A FOAM SPIKE

Foam is one of the most versatile materials in cosplay and entire books have been dedicated to its many uses. From detailed props to full-body armor, foam can form the foundation of countless costume elements. In this tutorial, we'll focus on creating a basic foam spike. It's a small but useful project that introduces key techniques. Once finished, the spike can be attached to garments with strong magnets, hot glue, or other methods depending on your needs. Think of this as a starting point: The skills you develop here can be applied to more complex foam builds down the line.

WHAT YOU WILL NEED

Template (page 145)

Tracing paper

Scissors

EVA foam, 5 mm

Chalk or pen

Cutting mat

X-ACTO knife

Heat gun

Respirator

Contact cement

Kwik Seal Caulk (optional)

Plasti Dip

Acrylic paint

Clear gloss spray enamel

1. Trace the template with tracing paper and then cut it out. (Or, you can make your own using the tutorial on page 143). Lay the template on top of the EVA foam. You can use the template you created, one purchased online, or the template we provided. Trace around the template with chalk or a pen.

2. Place the foam on a cutting mat. Cut out the template, making sure to cut the tip of the cone at a 45-degree angle.

3. Use a heat gun on the areas you cut.

4. Put on a respirator mask in a well-ventilated area. Spread a thin amount of contact cement on the seams that were cut at a 45-degree angle.

5. Wait until the contact cement is partially dry and ready to bond. It will be ready when it feels tacky and glossy.

6. Align the seams and press together, moving from one end to the other to avoid bubbles. Wait for the contact cement to fully cure.

7. (Optional) If you want to smooth the seam, use Kwik Seal Caulk.

8. Put on a respirator and spray the spike with Plasti Dip. I usually put the spike on a cardboard box to avoid making a mess. Allow the Plasti Dip to fully dry.

9. Paint the spike with acrylic paint in the color of your choice.

10. Once the paint is fully dry, go to a well-ventilated area and spray with clear gloss enamel to give the spike a glossy finish.

See final image on page 142.

TUTORIAL

CUSTOMIZING PREMADE HORNS

Cosplaying a character with horns can be tricky because a lot of horns have very specific shapes. There are endless ways to create these with methods such as clay or papier-mâché. Our preferred methods for making horns are either creating them from scratch via EVA foam or customizing premade foam horns!

If you don't want to worry about creating horns from scratch, buying and customizing horns is a great option. You can use your purchased horns as bases to create horns with a detailed handmade look. In this tutorial, we'll be covering parts of the horns in Worbla. Feel free to use what you learn from this process to customize further and get creative.

WHAT YOU WILL NEED

Store-bought horns

Plastic wrap

Duct tape

Marker

X-ACTO knife

Scissors

Worbla

Heat gun

Heat-resistant surface

Tip: Try wrapping a foam display board in metal insulation tape!

Wood burning tool and respirator (optional)

Gesso or wood glue

All-surface primer spray

Paint brushes or craft sponges

Acrylic paint

Silicone mat or parchment paper

Clear glossy acrylic coating spray (optional)

(continued)

CUSTOMIZING PREMADE HORNS (CONTINUED)

1. To create a pattern of your horn shape, wrap the horns in plastic wrap. Then wrap the horns in duct tape. I only plan on adding Worbla to the bottom of my horns, so I only wrapped the bottom of my horns.

2. Use a marker to draw outlines on the duct tape where you'll cut out the Worbla.

3. Cut off the duct tape using an X-ACTO knife. Then tidy up your pattern with scissors as needed.

4. Lay your pattern on your Worbla. Draw an outline with a marker or pencil. Then cut it out with scissors.

5. Use a heat gun to heat up your Worbla on a heat-resistant surface.

6. Once the Worbla has softened, wrap the Worbla around the horn.

7. (Optional) Put on a respirator mask and use a wood burning tool to carve texture into the Worbla.

8. Allow the Worbla to cool and then coat with Gesso or wood glue.

9. Wait until the glue is fully dry. Then, in a well-ventilated area, coat the horns in all-surface primer spray.

10. Wait for the primer to fully dry and then paint horns with acrylic paint. First layer on a solid color as the base coat, fully covering the primer.

11. Add extra dimension to your horns with thin layers of slightly lighter and darker shades than the base coat. Add darker shades in crevasses to exaggerate them.

12. Use the dry brush method to add highlights. Dip a stiff brush or dry sponge in a light shade of paint. Remove most of the paint by wiping the brush on a cloth. Lightly brush over raised areas and edges to create highlights.

13. (Optional) Once the paint is fully dry, go to a well-ventilated area and spray the horn with gloss enamel to give it a glossy finish.

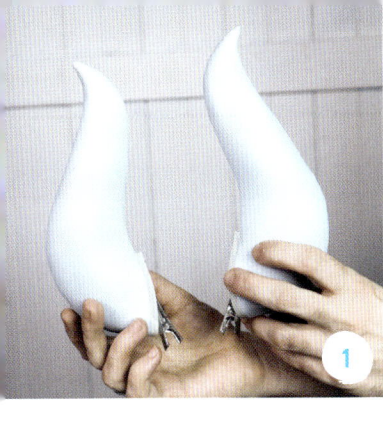

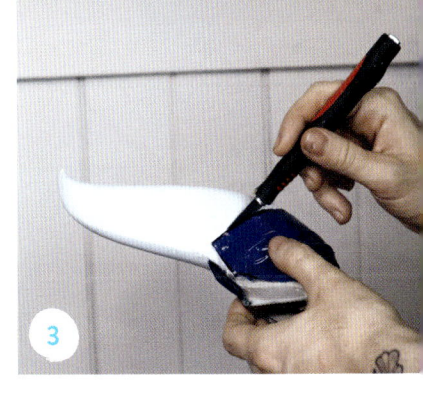

TUTORIAL

CUSTOMIZING A PROP SWORD

Making weapon props like swords from scratch can be very time consuming. If you need a sword for cosplay, an easier solution would be to buy a plastic toy sword and repaint it to suit your character. This can be a lot cheaper and save you time.

WHAT YOU WILL NEED

Plastic toy sword

Rubbing alcohol

Respirator

Paint primer

Painter's tape

Spray paint

Paint brushes

Acrylic paint

Gems and super glue (optional)

Spray enamel topcoat, matte or glossy

Leather straps (optional)

1. Clean the sword with rubbing alcohol. You want to remove all dust and particles from the sword before priming it to achieve a smoother base. If there are gems you want to replace, remove the old ones now.

2. Spray the primer onto one side at a time, allowing each side to dry completely before flipping the sword over. The number of coats required varies, but your primer should be completely opaque before you start painting. This could take around four coats. Make sure you wear your respirator any time you use spray paint.

(continued)

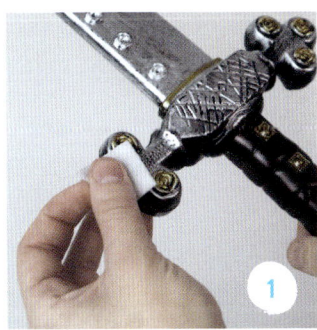

CUSTOMIZING A PROP SWORD (CONTINUED)

3. Tape the sword for painting. Using painter's tape, apply small pieces over any part of the sword that should not be painted. For this sword, only the blade will be silver, so I'm applying tape over the entirety of the grip, the cross guard, and the hilt.

4. Spray paint the blade, allowing each side to dry before moving it. This should take 2–3 layers.

5. Once the sword is completely dry, tape off the blade to protect the paint and repeat steps 3 and 4 for any other parts of the sword that need to be spray painted. For this sword, the cross guard and hilt will be spray painted with a gold base.

6. Remove all tape and begin using acrylic paint for the rest of the sword's base color. Use as many layers as necessary to create an opaque base.

7. Paint any small details onto the sword before weathering. If you are using gems, this is the time to glue them on with super glue.

8. Using darker colors than your base, apply a mixture of acrylic and water to any parts of the sword that should be weathered. Using a paper towel, pat these areas dry and smooth the color so that it looks natural. Repeat as many times as necessary to achieve the desired look. I want my sword to look like it's made of iron, so I am using a mixture of dark gray and rust colors.

9. Seal your paint with a topcoat enamel. This will prevent your paint from chipping as you walk around with it. For this sword, I'm using a matte enamel. If you want your sword to look silver or gold, try using a glossy enamel!

10 (Optional) Wrap the grip of the sword with a long leather strap and secure it with super glue.

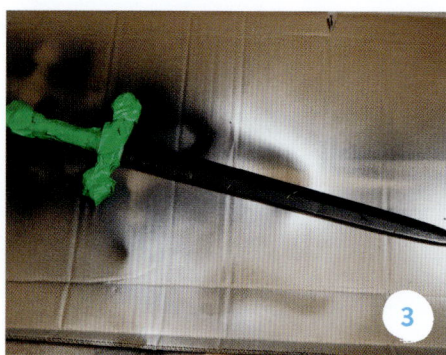
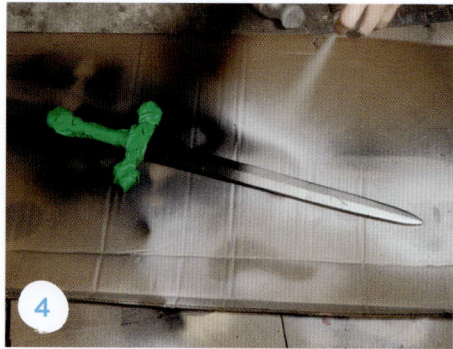

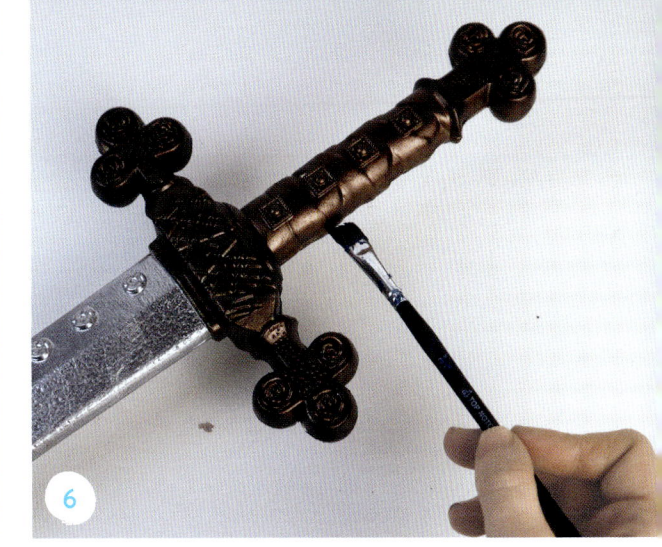

CRAFTING REALISTIC ANIMAL EARS

Animal ears can be bought cheaply from stores, but the affordable ears are often fairly low quality. Beautiful realistic ears that are made by artists tend to be rather expensive. With so many animal characters in existence, being able to craft your own high-quality animal ears is an incredibly useful skill. By following this tutorial, you'll be able to make your own realistic animal ears without any sewing skills whatsoever.

Shading Tips! Advanced Techniques for Future Mastery

Some people add shading to the inner parts of the ear for extra dimension and realism. The best and most permanent way to add shading is by using an airbrush. The simplest airbrush kits can be purchased online for around $30. You'll also need to buy paint that works with airbrushes. Make sure to practice using the airbrush on paper before using it to shade your ears.

If you don't have an airbrush, there are still ways to add shading to your ears. Some easy options are hair chalk, eyeshadow, or even pastels. Unfortunately, none of those methods are very permanent; they will fade with time. A more permanent method is to apply watered-down paint with a toothbrush. Make sure to only use a very small amount of paint on your toothbrush so it doesn't drip and ruin your ears. You're mimicking the effect of an airbrush, so you'll be applying only small amounts of paint lightly with the toothbrush.

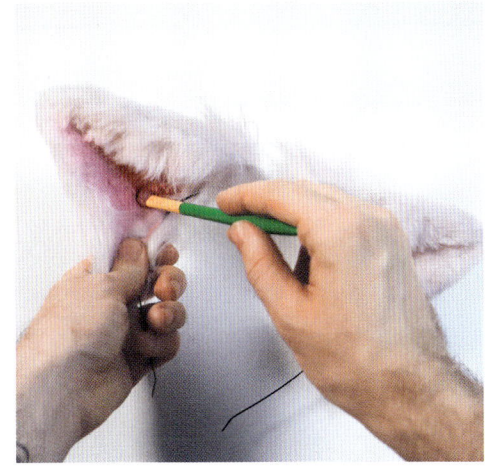

Shading

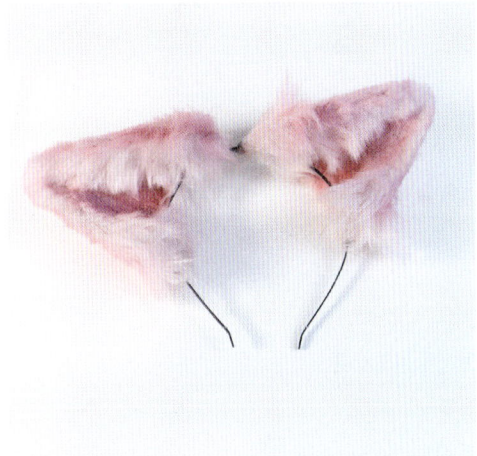

After Shading

TUTORIAL

ANIMAL EARS

Cosplay doesn't have to stick to human characters. There are so many fun creatures to try, such as monsters, animals, and hybrids. A lot of these characters have animal ears which can add tons of personality to your look. There are amazing artists online who sell high-quality ears that look beautiful and realistic, but making your own ears is also a great option! It can save you money, and you get to control exactly how they look. This tutorial will walk you through the basics and help you create a pair that's just right for your cosplay.

WHAT YOU WILL NEED

Pencil

Paper or cardstock

Scissors

Faux fur in the color of your choice

X-ACTO knife

EVA foam, 2 mm

Craft or sculpting aluminum wire mesh (optional)

Hot glue gun

12-gauge aluminum wire

Scissors

Electric clippers or shaver

Headband or hair clips

1. Start by drawing your pattern for your ears onto paper or cardstock. Paper is a great way to test your pattern cheaply. If you're not feeling confident with your own pattern, you can look online for patterns of various types of animal ears.

2. Cut out the pattern.

3. Hold the paper ear to your head. This will help you determine if you're happy with the ear's size and shape before proceeding.

4. Lay the fur cloth side up. Faux fur runs in one direction; make sure the hair is running upward.

5. Trace the pattern on the cloth side twice with a 1-cm margin. Flip the pattern and trace two more with a 1-cm margin. In total you should have four ear shapes drawn.

6. Cut out the ear shapes with an X-ACTO knife. Be careful to only cut the fabric and not the fur.

7. Use your pattern to draw and cut out one left ear shape and one right ear shape out of EVA foam.

8. (Optional) Use your pattern to cut out one left ear shape and one right ear shape out of aluminum wire mesh. Adding wire mesh will make your ears extra bendable and poseable. Hot glue the corresponding EVA foam and wire mesh pieces together.

(continued)

1

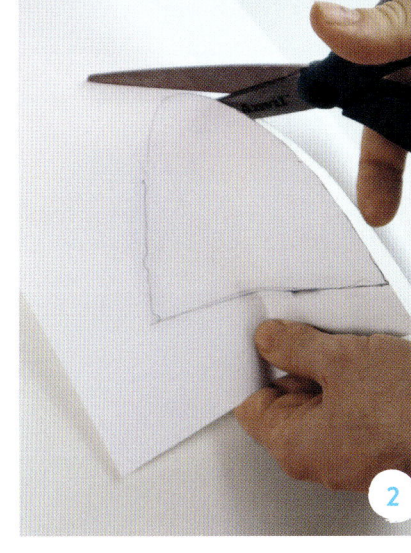
2

3

4

5

6

7

8a

8b

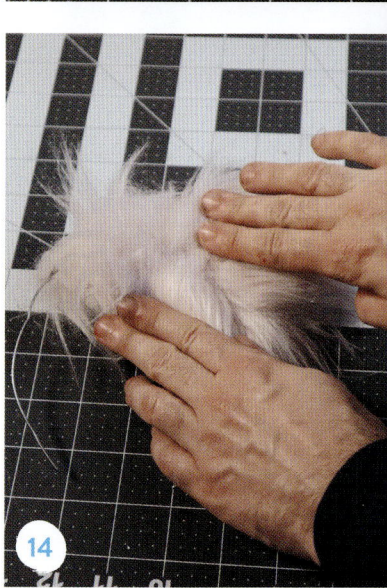

ANIMAL EARS (CONTINUED)

9. Take your 12-gauge aluminum wire and bend it into shape around the EVA foam ears. Leave two long pieces of wire poking out of the bottom. You will use these two long pieces to attach the ears to a headband later. If you plan on securing your ears with hair clips, you won't need these long pieces.

10. Apply hot glue to the foam, then press the wire into place to secure it around the edges.

11. Take the pieces of fur for the backs of the ears and apply hot glue over the surface.

12. Line up the fur with the foam-and-wire ears and press it on to join them. You have now attached the fur of the outer ears.

13. You have two unattached ear pieces left. These are for the inner ear. Apply hot glue around the exposed edges of the foam-and-wire ears and around the edges of the cloth side of the unattached ear pieces.

14. Carefully line up the inner fur ear pieces with the exposed inner parts of the foam-and-wire ears and press them into place, sandwiching the foam between the faux fur pieces.

15. Use scissors to carefully trim around the rough edges to tidy them up. Take care not to trim the fur when doing this.

16. Use your electric clippers to shave the fur. If you don't have electric clippers, you can use scissors instead. How you cut the fur will depend on the animal you are making and your intended style. Look at references for inspiration.

17. Push the hair around with your fingers to help separate the parts of fur you do and don't want to shave. This will help you avoid accidentally shortening fur that you want to keep long.

(continued)

ANIMAL EARS (CONTINUED)

18. For most animal ears, you'll shave the backs of the ears so that the tops are short and leave the bottoms longer.

19. For the insides of the ears, separate out some tufts of fur to keep long. You'll want long tufts of fur on the inner ear, where the ear folds over. You'll also want longer fur on the bottom outside side. Shave the top edges short. The very middle of the ear will be the shortest.

20. Use scissors to trim and tidy up the longer tufts.

21. Bend the ears into your desired shape.

22. Now you have your realistic animal ears! You can use the long pieces of wire to bend and wrap them around a headband. You can also choose to hot glue the ears to hair clips.

A FINAL WORD

Cosplay is an art and art is subjective. There are no right or wrong ways to design and create your look. What is important is that you enjoy yourself and are happy with what you make. Learning new skills is never easy—it takes a lot of trial and error. Cosplay is a great way to practice new techniques and express yourself in ways you never thought possible.

We hope that the small fraction of knowledge provided in this book can help jumpstart or reignite your journey into costumes, drag, and storytelling.

ACKNOWLEDGMENTS

We'd like to thank our families for supporting us on our cosplay journey. Kade's parents for supporting him through art school and providing the resources needed. Ken's mom for encouraging cosplay and telling her that nerds are cool. Grandma for teaching her how to sew. Papa would have loved to see this book on his shelf.

Thanks to our publishing team for working with us to create this book.

Special thanks to our wonderful supporters on Patreon who have made our journey possible.

Thank you to everyone who follows and subscribes to our cosplay channels; your encouragement and enthusiasm for our work keeps us going.

ABOUT THE AUTHORS

Ken is a cosplayer from Columbia, California. She first learned to sew when she lived with her grandmother when she was twelve years old. She was inspired by YouTube cosplay groups, who would dress up as characters and film skit-style videos and vlogs. At first, she cosplayed so she could enter and win cosplay competitions, but quickly realized her passion was with storytelling and cosplay content creation. Ever since then she's been cosplaying as a vessel to write and act out stories in video format.

Kade is a cosplayer from Ventura County, California. He has always loved anime, video games, and speculative fiction. His grandfather took him to San Diego Comic Con when he was just twelve years old, where he was inspired by the incredible cosplayers. Although he dabbled in cosplay as a teenager, he didn't begin pursuing it more seriously until his late twenties. At the time, he was working as a motion graphic designer and turned to cosplay as a creative outlet. He became especially drawn to the storytelling potential of short-form cosplay videos.

INDEX

A

Act One Costumes, 77

aging, makeup for, 84–87

airbrushes, 157

AliExpress, for costumes, 98

all-purpose dye, 99

Amazon, for wigs, 18

animal ears, 157–162

Arda Wigs, 18

B

bangs, trimming wig, 26–28

Barge All Purpose Cement, 136

BB creams, 42

beards

    coloring, long, 54

    coloring, products for, 53

    coloring, short, 57

    covering, 58–59

Ben Nye Aqua body paint, 80

Biotrue Multi-Purpose contact lens solution, 95

blackface, 80

blenders, beauty, 46

blood, 90

blush, 42–43, 49, 70, 75

body paint

    beards and, 53

    preparation for, 45

    types of, 80–81

    water-activated application, 83

Bold Hold Liquid Gold, 22, 24

bows, on footwear, 127

breasts, fake, 78

bronzers, 43, 49, 70

brushes, makeup, 44

burning, for weathering, 119

C

caps, wig, 21–22

cement, contact, 136

Cetaphil moisturizer, 45

characters, 11–14
    choosing, 12
    design traits of, 13
    original designs for, 14
color
    beards, 53, 54, 57
    fabric (see costume color customization)
    remover, costume, 99
    wigs and, 25, 36–37
combs, for wigs, 25
commissions, of costumes, 99
concealers, makeup
    about, 43
    for aging, 87
    for beard coverage, 58
    for drag makeup, 70, 75
    for eyebrow coverage, 62
    for feminine makeup, 46
contact lenses, 94–95
contouring
    about, 42
    for aging, 87
    for drag makeup, 70, 75
    for feminine makeup, 46–47
    for ghost makeup, 93
    for masculine makeup, 52, 75

corsets and hip pads, 79
Coscom Cosplay Supplies, 136
cosplay
    about, 9
    character development, 11–14 (see also characters)
    costumes for, 97–133 (see also costumes)
    makeup for, 41–95 (see also makeup)
    props for, 135–162 (see also props)
    wigs for, 17–38 (see also wigs)
costume color customization
    of leather, 106
    ombré, 102–103
    products for, 99
    staining, 119
    on stovetop, 101
    in washing machine, 104–105
costumes, 97–133
    buying, 98–99
    fabric color, customization of (see costume color customization)
    fabric paint and, 107–111
    footwear (see footwear)
    iron-ons and (see iron-ons)
    patches and, 115
    spikes on, 123–125

symbols on, 108–109

vinyl, iron-on, 116–117

weathering, 119–121

Covergirl foundations, 45

cream body paint, 80

Cricut machines, 116

crowns, 139–141

curling, of wigs, 30–31

D

design traits, of characters, 13

detangling spray, for wigs, 25

Diamond FX body paint, 80

distressing, of costumes, 123–125

DokiDoki Cosplay, for costumes, 98

drag makeup

about, 61

eyebrows, 61–63, 76

eyelashes, 68

eyes, exaggerated, 64–67

face, 70–71, 75

facial hair, 77

gems, 69

king, 75–79

lips, 72

prosthetics, 78–79

dremels, 136

DUO lash glue, 44

dyeing

fabric (see costume color customization)

wigs, 25, 36–37

E

ears, animal, 157–162

Ebay, for costumes, 98

e.l.f. Power Grip Primer, 45

enamel topcoats, 137

Epic Cosplay, 18

EVA foam. See foam work

eyebrow pomade, 53, 57, 93

eyeliners

about, 43

for exaggerated eyes, 64–65, 67

for feminine makeup, 49

for ghost makeup, 93

eye makeup

exaggerated, 64–67

eyebrows, 52, 61–63, 76, 93

eyeliners (see eyeliners)

eyeshadow (see eyeshadow)

instructions for, 48–49

lashes, 44, 67, 68

mascara, 49, 65, 67

eyeshadow

    about, 43

    for aging, 87

    for beard coloring, 53, 54, 57

    for exaggerated eyes, 64, 66–67

    for facial hair, 77

    for feminine makeup, 48

    for ghost creation, 93

    for masculine makeup, 52, 76

    for scar creation, 88

EZcosplay, for costumes, 98

F

fabric

    color, changing of (see costume color customization)

    fraying, 119

    paint, 107–110

    staining, 119

    transfers, 113–114

facial hair, 24, 77. See also beards

feminine makeup techniques, 46–50

Five Wits Wigs, 18

foam work, 136–137. See also props

footwear

    detail additions, 127

    glitter, 128–129

    painting, 132–133

    ribbons, 130–131

foundations

    about, 42

    for beard coverage, 58

    colored, 81

    for drag makeup, 70, 75

    techniques, 45–46

fraying fabric, 119

Fusion Body Art, 80

G

gems

    face, 69

    footwear, 127

gender-bending, 14

ghosts, makeup for, 91–95

glitter, on footwear, 128–129

glue

    for eyebrows, 61–63

    for face gems, 69

    for facial hair, 24, 77

    for foam work, 136, 137

    for footwear, 127, 129, 130

    for glitter, 129

    hot glue guns, 137

    for lashes, 44, 68

    for wigs, 22–23, 24, 25

Got2Be Glued, 25

grease body paint, 80

H

hair. See wigs

hair crimper, 25

hairspray, wigs and, 25

hair wax, beards and, 53, 54

heat guns, 136

highlighter, makeup, 49, 67, 70, 87, 93

hip pads and corsets, 79

horns, 149–151

hot glue guns, 137

I

iron-ons

    about, 112

    fabric transfers, 113–114

    patches, 115

    vinyl, 116–117

J

jackets, spikes on, 124–125

K

Kasou Wig, 18

King Boo (Super Mario Bros.), 14

KVD Good Apple Foundation, 45

Kwik Seal, 136

L

lashes, false, 44, 68. See also mascara

leather, weathering of fake, 120–121

leather dye, 99, 106

Link (Legend of Zelda), 13

lip makeup

    for drag, 72

    for ghost creation, 93

    types of, 50

liquid body paint, 81

M

makeup, 41–95

    about, 41

    aging with, 84–87

    beards and, 54, 57, 58–59

    drag (see drag makeup)

    eye (see eye makeup)

    for ghosts, 91–95

    lip, 50, 72

    preparation for, 45–46

    products for, 42–44

    scars, 88–90

    special effects (SFX) (see SFX makeup)

    techniques, feminine, 46–50

    techniques, masculine, 52–59

Mane 'n Tail detangler, 25

Mario (Mario franchise), 106

mascara, 93

masculine makeup techniques, 52–59

Maybelline foundations, 45

Mehron Paradise body paint, 80, 91

Mercari, for costumes, 98

Miccostumes, 98

Mod Podge, 137

Monokuma (Danganronpa franchise), 14

Morphe Continuous Mist setting spray, 44

muscle suits, 78

O

Olay moisturizer, 45

ombré dyeing, costume, 102–103

P

paint

    body (see body paint)

    fabric, 107–111

    for foam work, 137

    for footwear, 132–133

    spray, 137

patches, 115

Pinky Paradise, for colored contacts, 94

Plasti Dip, 137

pleather, weathering of, 120–121

pomade, eyebrow, 53, 57

primers, makeup, 42, 45–46

Princess Peach (Mario franchise), 13

props, 135–162

    about foam work, 136–137

    animal ears, 157–162

    crowns, 139

    horns, 149–151

    spikes, 142–147

    swords, 153–155

Pros-Aide, 77

prosthetics, 78–79

purchasing tips

    costumes, 98–99

    makeup, 42–44

    wigs, 18

R

respirators, 136

ribbons, on footwear, 130–131

rigid collodion, 88

Rin Kagamine (Vocaloid), 13

Rit fabric dye, 25

rubbing alcohol, for cleaning wigs, 38

S

sandpaper, for weathering, 119

scars, makeup for, 88–90

scissors, 25

setting, makeup, 44

SFX makeup

    aging, 84–87

    body paint, water-activated, 83

    ghost, 91–95

    scars, 88–90

shoes. See footwear

sideburns, 24

silhouetting, for drag, 78–79

Smitizen, 78

Snazaroo body paint, 80

Softmary Breastplate, 78

Sora (Kingdom Hearts), 33

special effects (SFX). See SFX makeup

spikes

    on costumes, 123–125

    foam props, making, 142–147

    on wigs, 33–35, 38

Spirit Halloween, 99

spray paint, 137

stains, creating for costume, 119

steamers, for wigs, 25

stovetop dyeing, costume, 101

styling tools, for wigs, 25

swords, 153–155

symbols, on costumes, 107–109

synthetic dye, 99

T

Tarte Face Tape Foundation, 45

tea/coffee staining, costumes, 119

Temu, for costumes, 98

torn fabric, 119

tutorials

- beards, coloring, 54, 57
- beards, covering, 58–59
- costumes, fabric transfers, 113–114
- costumes, iron-on vinyl, 116–117
- costumes, leather spikes and, 124–125
- costumes, patches, 115
- costumes, symbols with fabric paint, 108–109
- costumes, weathering, 120–121
- fabric dyeing, in washing machine, 104–105
- fabric dyeing, leather, 106

fabric dyeing, ombré, 102–103, 110–111

fabric dyeing, on stovetop, 101

footwear, detail additions, 127

footwear, glitter, 128–129

footwear, painting, 132–133

footwear, ribbons, 130–131

makeup, aging with, 84–87

makeup, ghost, 91–95

makeup, scars, 88–90

makeup, water-activated body paint, 83

props, animal ears, 157–162

props, crowns, 139–141

props, horns, 149–151

props, spikes, 146–147

props, spike templates, 143–145

props, swords, 153–155

wigs, bang trimming, 26–28

wigs, curling, 30–31

wigs, dyeing, 36–37

wigs, putting on, 23–24

wigs, spikes on, 33–35

wigs, volume of, 29

V

vinyl, iron-on, 116–117

W

Walmart, for costumes, 99

washing machine dyeing, costume, 104–105

water-activated body paint, 80, 83

weathering, of costumes, 119–121

Weekendwigs, 18

wefts, of wigs, 20

Weldwood Original Contact Cement, 136

wig heads, 25

wigs, 17–38

    bang trimming, 26–28

    buying tips, 18

    caps, 21–22

    curling, 30–31

    dyeing, 36–37

    maintenance and storage of, 38

    putting on, 23–24

    quality of, 20

    spike formation on, 33–35

    styling, about, 25

    types of, 19

    volume, adding, 29

Wig Is Fashion, 18

Wish, for costumes, 98

Worbla, 137

wrinkles, creating, 87

X

X-ACTO knives, 136

Y

Yugi (Yi-Gi-Oh!), 33